Getting in Touch with Your Inner Rich Kid

The Not-So-Rich Kid's Guide to the Emotions of Money and Wealth

978-0-9792901-9-0

Justin Locke

978-0-9792901-9-0

(Version 3.0)
Printed in the USA

Published by

Justin Locke Productions
Lincoln, Massachusetts

www.justinlocke.com

Also by Justin Locke:

Real Men Don't Rehearse
(*Adventures in the Secret World*
of Professional Orchestras)

Principles of Applied Stupidity
(*How to Get and Do More by*
Thinking and Knowing Less)

Time Light Love
Exploring the Physics of Emotional Energy

Family Concert Works:

Peter VS. the Wolf
(For orchestra and five actors; music by Prokofiev)

The Phantom of the Orchestra
(*or, the Dark Side of the Symphony*)
(For orchestra and five actors)

Introduction

If you walk into a bookstore or a library, you will find thousands of books that will tell you how to make more money. And if you already have lots of money, there are thousands of books that will tell you how to manage your money in such a way that you will make even more money.

But in this massive sea of financial advice, there is one essential item missing, and that is:

How to not . . . push money away from you.

This may strike you as being a rather unnecessary skill. Who would push money away from themselves? Well, fact is, lots of people do. Let's get right to the point: some of us grow up as members of an oppressed class. If you did, then you learned a system of values and rules that rationalized your getting less money than other people. If your parents were poor, if you go out and make money you are being disloyal to them. This training lies deep in the subconscious, and unless you recognize it and deal with it, it will forever sabotage your best efforts to achieve happiness and financial success. It is more emotional than logical, and has to be dealt with on that level.

If you grew up in poverty, or if you have experienced the emotional/physical trauma that a lack of cash can cause, you may have created internal thought systems that helped you to cope with going without. You may have come to believe that rich people are evil, and being poor is noble. You may think people who work hard are suckers, and it's foolish to buy anything but the cheapest car or clothes. The list goes on and on. In a class based system, it is actually essential to make those in the lower classes believe they are somehow morally better than those who have all the money, as otherwise pitchforks and torches would be the norm. In other words, you may be a victim of a kind of brainwashing that we shall hereafter refer to as "poor kid thinking."

Just to list some common examples: you may know at least one successful person who "grew up poor," and now, even though they have lots of money, they can't bring themselves to spend any of it. You may know someone who is talented and dedicated, and yet success eludes them; they hesitate to charge anything for their services, because they can't imagine anyone else feeling any desire for their work. And have you ever tried to give someone a gift, only to have it rejected because they felt they did not "deserve something so nice"? If so, then you have seen the blocked energy of "poor kid thinking" at work. And that's just the beginning.

So here you have a slightly different "money management" book. Unlike most books on handling money, this one is not about arithmetic, nor is it about monthly budgets, compound interest, or capital gains. Instead, it's about managing the emotional issues of money, especially those resulting from growing up without it. It is about the confusion that can occur in your subconscious mind regarding money, and how we often get it mixed up with other issues of personal interactions. It is about exposing habits that were originally created to help you survive a difficult situation, but may now be preventing you from achieving the happiness and success you seek. It's about starting a process of self discovery, and healing the trauma of growing up in a "scarcity environment." It asks far more questions than it answers, but it places faith in you to find the answer that is right for you.

Most books on wealth and abundance try to cultivate a positive outlook and emotional state. That kind of thing is very important. This book, sad to say, does not do that. It is more in the realm of going to the dentist. It is not terribly uplifting, and at times may be a little bit painful. The goal is to bring negative issues up to the light where they can be faced, healed, and discarded. Hopefully you will only need to read it once, and by finally addressing and releasing your hidden anchors of past money trauma, it will make the books that have purely positive messages be more effective for you.

Everyone is born with an optimistic outlook and an enormous capacity for love, trust, cooperation, and generosity, but many of us lose sight of this immense potential because somewhere along the line, someone taught us to think like "poor kids." If this happened to you, this book will hopefully serve to get you back in touch with your "inner rich kid."

1

Internalized Oppression

Candidates for political office often state that they "want everyone to be rich." This is a lovely sentiment, but it is impossible to execute. If you have ever wondered why poverty persists despite all our efforts and stated desire to end it, there is an obvious reason for why this is: monetary wealth is relative, and in order for some people to be rich, you have to have other people who are poor. If poor people did not exist, people who want to be rich would have to create them. And throughout history, that is exactly what has been done.

Now if you are on the poor person end of the stick here, it is very easy to blame all of your troubles on these abusive carpet-bagging rich people. But this is only one side of the story. Yes, there have always been efforts to exploit and oppress large numbers of people, but it is very hard to oppress large numbers of people for very long unless you can somehow convince them to accept their state of being oppressed. This is where "poor kid thinking" becomes so important.

"Poor kid thinking" is not an individual shortcoming. Instead, it is a broad cultural phenomenon. A lot of it comes from the outside, but a lot of it is also self-induced.

If you were born into a "scarcity environment" (resulting from mismanagement, economic/political oppression, or maybe just a dry climate), well, let's face it, you didn't have much in the way of choices or options. Not only were you constantly having to come up with workarounds just to survive, you were also surrounded by people who were coping with those same privations themselves. This collective and/or inherited "survival mode" – in both physical and psychic terms– may have become an accepted way of life. If your neighbors and your family all fell into this system, well, in your natural eagerness to "fit in" and be accepted by your group (and, being primates, acceptance by the group is awfully important to all of us), it's hard to not fall into the culture of "poor kid thinking" along with everyone else. And once you fall into "poor kid thinking," the "rich people" don't have to do very much to oppress you any more, as you are now unwittingly doing it to yourself.

Many books have been written about how the "lower classes" and poor people in general are victims of oppression. Yes, that is a big part of the story, but it's not the whole story. Assigning all the blame on someone else blinds us to the many ways in which one's own "poor kid thinking" serves to perpetuate one's being poor. This "poor-kid" cultural training, which reinforces behaviors that maintain a state of impoverishment, is just as much to blame as any outside influence. You have the power to climb out of your financial difficulties, but your "poor kid thinking' is a figurative wedding guest without a garment, sabotaging you from within, telling you that you don't have this power. This book will hopefully show you how to recognize these symptoms and rid yourself of them.

As the saying goes, "if you can't beat them, join them," and this book is about leaving the cultural values of "poor kids" behind and joining the ranks of the "rich kids." It would be nice if the oppressors in your life would have a change of heart, and create policies that would lift poor people like you out of poverty, but, as previously stated, they have no motivation to do so. Even if they did, "poor kid thinking" is highly resistant to accepting any help in becoming rich. So let's scale back a bit, and instead of thinking about painful history or grand government policy, let's focus solely on you, and what you have the power to change here and now. Let's undo your "poor kid" training, and start turning you back into the "rich kid" you were meant to be.

2

How We Learn to See Wealth as Being Evil

One of the classic ways that "poor kids" are taught to push money away from themselves is the oh-so-common insinuation that people who have a lot of money are evil. Certainly, if money (and the people who have it) is seen as being evil, both by you and by everyone you know, you are far less likely to want to become rich yourself. How do we learn to think of money this way? Well . . .

You might think of money as being wonderful, but that's mostly when you think about getting it yourself. When other people have it and you don't, suddenly it's not so wonderful. We all suffer from envy from time to time, but when you don't have any money for a long period of time and you constantly see other people who are well off all the time, it's natural to start feeling angry or resentful.

If you have this anger or resentment, you may have a desire to vent it somehow. And those wonderful folks in Hollywood know there is a lot of money to be made in giving you a place to vent your anger and resentment. They do this by giving you an image of a really nasty, evil, rich person to hate.

There are lots of wealthy bad guys in the movies– Mr. Potter, Mr. Burns, Noah Cross, Gordon Gekko, Caledon

Hockley, too many to count really– but perhaps the most obvious are the villains in James Bond movies. There are many different James Bond movie villains of course, but they all pretty much have one thing in common: they are all billionaire industrialists.

Billionaire industrialists tend to get a bad rap in the movies. Granted, in real life, billionaire industrialists are human, hence none of them are perfect, and it's certainly true that there has been more than one occasional bad apple here and there. But let's face it: without the people who create and run these major corporate entities, most of us would be living in subsistence farming communities. Some of these billionaires may be evil mega-maniacal geniuses, and they may be bent on world domination, but on the plus side, they do provide an awful lot of nifty products, and they also provide employment for millions of people. Hey, there's always a trade-off.

Sadly, the movies don't offer much in the way of a balanced viewpoint. It's not like they bother to offer any mitigating circumstances to excuse these bad guys' narcissistic behavior, like maybe mentioning their having been toilet trained too early. Nope. Instead, the average James Bond movie places an enormous amount of emphasis on the villain's whole "bent on world domination" aspect of their personality, and maybe a similar emphasis on their bizarre sexual preferences. In fact, these billionaire James Bond movie villains have no redeeming features whatsoever. They are shown as being completely black hearted, evil to the core, and, well, just generally not a very nice person. Certainly not someone you would invite over for Sunday dinner.

So here's the question: given the fact that rich people are generally portrayed in the movies as being consistently loathsome and objectionable, would you ever want to be like them? That is to say, would you ever in a million years want other people to feel about you the way you feel about these fat cat rich people? Of course not. And since there is a subtle but consistent message that people with a lot of money are all just as immoral, lonely, evil, perverse, and not nice to their mothers as these James Bond villains, it is reasonable to ask yourself, "Who in their right mind would want to be like these awful people?"

Now on the flip side, consider the good guy. James Bond is just utterly awesome in every way. Of course, he's not rich; he's just a salaried government employee. He probably makes less money than you do. He devotes most of his time (both on and off the job) to gambling, alcohol, firearms, expensive gadgets, fast cars, and loose women. He employs no one, and by the way, all of his activities, gadgets, and fast cars are paid for entirely by the taxpayers.

The upshot of all this is, we are all encouraged to hate the guy who is imaginative, industrious, goal oriented, and an employer. And the hero, the one we are encouraged to admire and emulate, is just one more working stiff with a government job and an annoying boss. And unlike the rich guy, Mr. Bond gets the admiration of the general public, not to mention a nonstop series of romps in the sack with absolutely gorgeous women.

So when that day comes when you have an opportunity to make more money than you do now, well, it may not occur to you on a conscious level, but somewhere, you may be asking yourself, "Will taking this higher paying job make me an object of disgust and hatred in the eyes of the entire universe?" After watching all these movies, you may, without ever thinking about it, have an automatic reflex in your heart that says, "To have a lot of money is to be immoral and despised." So when push comes to shove, you may feel emotionally conflicted. You might pass up the opportunity to improve yourself, not for any logical reason, but because these movies, and the constant demonizing of wealthy people in the popular culture in general, have led you to feel that having more money is somehow immoral.

3

What Is Money, Anyway?

There are lots of books and TV shows about money, and lots of people telling you how to spend your money, how to make more money, and how to invest your money. But has anyone ever taken their focus off lecturing you about your money long enough to try explain to just what exactly it is that we're talking about?

If not, well, it's time. He we go. The best way to explain it is to tell you a story.

Once upon a time there was a woman who dealt in "collectibles," which is a nice way of saying she was a junk dealer. In the pre-Ebay era, she would seek out garage and yard sales, and buy all sorts of old used items. She would then re-sell them at weekend flea markets, at a tidy profit.

Amidst her odd and sundry inventory, she always had a box of old postcards. This was a fairly standard item offered by all of her junk-dealing colleagues. Throughout the flea market, at every table, you would see a box of old postcards. Most of the dealers offered them at a price of 25 cents apiece.

This lady, however, had a different approach. She priced her postcards, not at 25 cents, but at $5 apiece.

The other junk dealers all scoffed at her for asking this outlandish price. "Who will buy an old postcard for $5?" they would ask. "They hardly ever buy them even for a quarter."

Now at this point, yes, one might think this was either an extreme case of wishful thinking, or perhaps a use of the old "higher price equals higher quality" marketing ploy . . . but even that tried-and-true method was probably not going to work with this box of old, used, ragged, stained, dog-eared, moldy postcards.

So when she was asked why she priced them that way, she replied:

"Price is not an issue here. You could price these postcards at a penny apiece or even offer them for free, and most people would not be interested at all. *But*," she said, "if one of these old postcards has a picture of the house you grew up in, you'll pay $5 or even $10 for it. If you really want it, *money is no object*."

Every now and then we hear this phrase, that "money is no object," meaning we are willing to pay whatever the asking price is. But when we parse it out further, there is something rather intriguing in both of the clauses of this phrase: "If you really want it . . . money is no object."

The first step in learning to manage money is to understand that money is not an "object." It never was, and never will be. Money is occasionally "expressed" in paper or metal form, but the vast majority of the "money" in the world does not exist in any tangible form whatsoever. Less than 15% of the American "money supply" exists as gold, coins, or paper. The rest of it is just numbers stored in a computer somewhere. It is not an "object" in a physical sense. And even the "value" of "cold hard cash" goes up and down, depending on various market factors.

So if money is not an object, if it is not coins or ingots or pieces of paper, then what is it?

For the answer, the first clause, "If you really want it," tells us much.

At its most basic level, money is simply *a number that we ascribe to our desires*. It is a number that expresses how much you want something.

Money is also a number that expresses what you don't want. If you don't want to change your spark plugs, or if you don't want to die of appendicitis, then there are certain amounts of money that you are willing to give away to avoid those outcomes. That amount of money indicates the level of desire you have. The idea of "price" being based on "supply and demand" is really about "supply and desire."

So whenever we talk about money, we always have to somehow reconcile the money, i.e., a purely numerical concept, with the not-so-numerical emotions/desires it represents. There is no such thing as "intrinsic value." The value of things is based entirely on the current amount of human desire for them. Understanding the emotions of desire– yours and everyone else's– is key to understanding money. It's as much poetry as it is paper.

4

Desire Defined

Now that we have established that money is a number we assign to desire, the next question is: what do you desire?

This is a broad topic, but before we go any further, there is a common presumption that should be addressed. There was once a fellow named Maslow who came up with various theories about the priorities of human needs and desires, and this is usually expressed in a pyramid, with basic physiological needs being shown as the primary desire of human beings. Everyone is entitled to their opinion, but with all due respect to Mr. Maslow, he got it all wrong. Physiological needs are important, but love and connection are way more important than anything else.

All else is secondary to love and connection. People will give up food, sex, even life itself, to maintain a sense of connection and belonging. The worst thing you can do to a prison inmate, even worse than the threat of death, is to put them in solitary confinement where they are denied any connection.

We hear stock market reports every day, and paychecks are always nice, but there are very few songs written about either one. Money is not where our primary emotional energy resides. We are far more interested in interpersonal connections than we are in money.

Social connections have many categories and labels. The most powerful of these is referred to as "love." Of course, we live in a world where the word "love" has become a euphemism for sex, so we should be very specific here, and say we will define "love" as a sense of interpersonal connection. It has many poetic synonyms– e.g., belonging, family, togetherness, membership . . . but whatever you call it, it is our highest priority.

We seek connection first and foremost. That is our greatest desire. Since this is a book about desire, that needed to be said. Once we have our desire for connection satisfied, we go on to lesser desires, but this is a book about desire, and it is based on the premise that we desire connection ahead of all other things. We desire other material things of course, but no matter what your desires may be, it's important to keep track of them. It is desire, and the cultivation or the suppression of it (not a collection of vague external mathematical formulae), that lead to wealth or poverty.

Now when someone says or thinks that they have a desire for money, this is somewhat skewed. Anyone who desires money is crazy. After all, if I gave you a million one-dollar bills, that would be nothing more than a pile of dirty paper taking up space. Where so much confusion begins is thinking that money has "intrinsic value." It doesn't. *Money only has value because it can be exchanged for things that you want.* Many people have a Pavlovian response to money because we associate money with the things we want, just as Pavlov's dogs associated the bell with food. They couldn't eat the bell, and you can't eat the money.

So if you seek only to accumulate money, that's just odd. It's like buying lots of power tools but never building anything with them.

Money is a tool, a means to another end, i.e., of getting what you desire. So again, the question becomes, what do you truly desire? We all want many different things, but more than anything else, we all seek love and connection.

This book is all about how money represents desire, so it is important to keep these words defined and these thoughts organized.

5

For Poor Kids, Desire is Bad

Okay, before we go any further, since money is a reflection of desire, let's talk a little bit about poor kids and desire.

Imagine, if you will, the following scenario: you go into a supermarket or a drugstore, you pick up whatever it is you want to buy, and you're minding your own business, just standing in the checkout line. And just ahead of you in line is a young mother (or father) with a toddler in tow.

Now of course, at these checkout line areas, you are more or less stuck there, waiting your turn. And as you stand there with nowhere else to go, you are confronted with thousands of boxes of candy bars. Here is all this wonderful chocolate and sugar, wrapped in brightly colored packages, decorated with smiling welcoming faces.

These oh-so-tempting treats are all stacked up, not behind the counter, not up at eye level, but in a seemingly inconvenient location, from floor level to knee level, where you have to stoop to pick them up. But as luck may have it, this inconvenient bend-over-to-get-it shelf space just happens to be in prime visual and grabbing space for any toddler whose parent is stuck waiting in the line. What a coincidence. And even more of a coincidence is that virtually every drug and convenience store has this exact same checkout-line setup.

Well, you know what's coming. The parent is stuck in line with the kid, the kid has precious little to do except survey this vast treasure of sugary treats, and of course a massive desire for one of these treats inevitably manifests itself. The kid then either asks for one of these treats or just grabs it. The parent then intercedes and says, "No, you can't have that." And at this point, you are of course grabbing for your earplugs, because everyone in the checkout line is about to be treated to a hundred-decibel demonstration of what it feels like to sincerely and urgently want something, and not be allowed to have it.

The reason for sharing this rather unpleasant and all too familiar story with you is this: it illustrates just how painful it is to be presented with something in a way that makes you want it desperately, and then, just as you reach for it or ask for it, to be told you can't have it. Granted, as we get older, we don't yell quite so loud, but the feeling stays more or less the same.

Now you would think . . . and it would be logical to assume . . . that kids who grow up poor would have greater desire than kids who grow up rich. After all, poor kids have consistently gotten less throughout their little lives, so you would think that when they get to adulthood, all that pent-up unfulfilled desire would manifest itself in a nonstop shopping spree. And on the flip side, it would be logical for you to think that the rich kids would be fully satisfied with all the stuff that they already have, and thus have less desire generally..

Sadly, you would be wrong.

For poor kids, it's not just the candy bars that they want and don't get. It's everything from shoes to food to love. Since poor kids are repeatedly and chronically told that they can't have things that they want (and more importantly, they are often told that they cannot have many of the things that they desperately *need*), they start to develop survival mechanisms. They start to figure out ways to stop the pain of these (what we shall hereafter call) "refusal experiences." A number of ingenious methodologies are created and employed to this end. Sad to say, children of scarcity usually figure out that the best way to avoid a "refusal experience" is to simply not want or need things in the first place. By suppressing their desires, they lessen the number of these painful refusal experiences, and regain some sense of control over their lives.

And of course, since money is a number that we assign to desire, if you decide you need to suppress your desire, you are going to have to suppress anything and everything associated with it. This means money itself has to be suppressed as well, since money is just a number assigned to desire. And as the natural inclination to avoid painful feelings leads to the suppression of desire, we start to see the cancerous growth of "poor kid thinking."

6

Universal Limitation and General Negativity

Along with "desire is bad," there are two other key elements of "poor kid thinking." These are:

The Belief in Universal Limitation and

The Presumption of General Negativity.

To explain where these concepts come from, consider the following scenario:

Let's say you are one of three small children. You are the oldest, and you have a younger sister and an even younger brother. And one night, when you have all seated yourselves at the dinner table, uh oh, something's wrong. You look around and you see that there are only two chicken leg drumsticks for the three of you. For whatever reason, you are suddenly dealing with a scarcity environment. There isn't enough, What to do?

Now at this point, dear reader, you may immediately say, "Well, just cut them up in such a way that everybody gets an equal share." That is an excellent idea, and it is evidence of your inner rich kid speaking. But what if such "fairness" . . . is somehow lacking? What if mom and dad are still at work, or the babysitter isn't paying much attention? What if baby brother has already eaten one of the drumsticks without asking or thinking about it?

If this is the case, anxiety is immediately established, as things are no longer "fair," and there is now a high likelihood that someone will go without altogether. Even if you manage to nab the last drumstick for yourself, okay, you got fed, but now you have to live with the guilt of your baby sister going hungry. There is no happy ending available to you. You just can't win.

This would be bad enough as a one-time event, but what if this kind of mismanagement is occurring night after night?

(Bear in mind, while we are using chicken legs to illustrate this concept, this could be about anything that is in short supply in your life, such as love, honesty, respect, personal safety, recognition of your abilities, opportunities for advancement, and so on.)

Your first reaction to chronic scarcity may be anger and resentment. But if those emotions don't elicit an acceptable fix from higher authority, and if the problem tends to repeat again and again, well, after a while, the pain and stress get to be just too much to bear. At some point you must somehow rationalize, i.e., *make sense of*, this irrational nonsensical situation. You must develop some kind of overall management theory that will allow you to gain some command and control of the situation.

A common approach is to simply accept the situation, and convince yourself that the scarcity (that appears to be the cause of the conflict) is normal. Once this approach is adopted, after a while, to save time, you just start to assume that there are limited amounts of just about everything. And of course, if the universe is a place of constant scarcity, well, it is very easy to conclude that the world is a pretty negative place in general. Once you do that, the injustice can't surprise you anymore, so now the injustice is not so hard to take when it happens.

And thus, these two elements of poor kid thinking– the belief in both universal limitation and general negativity– are created.

Bear in mind, poor kid thinking is the result of very good intentions. It is created in an attempt to fix a problem. Unfortunately, it actually serves to perpetuate it.

The real issue here is not one of scarcity; that's just a symptom. The real issue is the injustice and the lies. A lack of resources by itself does not equal being in a state of poverty. Everyone has "downturns" here and there. The "poor kid thinking" comes from believing that scarcity of resources (and the unjust distribution of them) is inevitable, inescapable, and constant. One then builds an approach to life based on these negative expectations. You are conditioned to assume that no matter what you do, "there will never be enough." And if you are always expecting scarcity and injustice, you will tend to manifest that energy in your life without realizing it.

There are many possible causes of (and psychological responses to) constant scarcity, but these three presumptions– desire is bad, there are limited amounts of everything, and this is a negative universe– form the core

27

of poor kid thinking. That's the basic theory. (There are also the common poor kid responses of fear, anger, mistrust, and resentment– we'll get to those later). So let's start to undo this "poor kid" training by juxtaposing it with the wealth-minded attitudes of "rich kids."

7

Poor Kid, Rich Kid

Once upon a time there was a kid who was, well, for want of a better word, poor. There are varying degrees of poor, and this kid was way better off than some of his even poorer poor kid friends (some of whom lived in true dirt floor squalor). But even so, this kid still had the core poor kid experience of largely going without. He was lucky to scrape by with the bare minimum of just about everything, including food, warmth, clothing, pocket change, and love.

This poor kid lived in a poor community, and so he of course attended the local poor kid school. He took classes with all the other poor kids of that poor neighborhood. The school had the requisite state requirements of classes and teachers, but to be honest, there was little expectation that any of these kids would be bettering their lives anytime soon. Like so many other aspects of their lives, everything in that poor school world was the bare minimum; it had the lowest paid teachers, the cheapest books, and so on.

But as fate may have it, one day the planets aligned in such a way that this poor kid had a chance to leave this poor kid school, and attend the local rich kid private school. He did not ask for it– poor kids never do. In fact he had simply dropped out of school and expected no one to notice. But someone did notice, and soon thereafter some scholarship money magically appeared. Thus, this poor kid found himself stepping through the looking glass into a whole new rich kid world, the likes of which he had never imagined.

So let us follow him on his adventure, and see what we can learn about poverty and wealth by comparing the worlds of poor kids and rich kids.

8

Poor Kids and Trust

When this poor kid went from the poor kid school to the rich kid school, the difference was extreme and immediately apparent, and yet it was not obvious just exactly what that difference was. In a purely physical dimension, this rich kid school was not terribly different from the poor kid school. There were teachers and students, there were classrooms and lockers.

But there was, in fact, one massive overriding difference between the poor kid school and the rich kid school, and this was . . . trust. Simply stated, the rich kid school operated on a system of trust, while in the poor kid school, there just wasn't any.

In the poor kid school, the daily routine didn't really have the look and feel of an academic institution. It was more like a prison camp. Head counts were constantly taken, and your presence was tracked at all times. "Cutting class" was a serious offense, although there wasn't much point in doing it, as there was nowhere to go. If you wished to leave a classroom legally, this required seeking written permission from someone in authority over you. If your request was deemed to be reasonable (and this only came about after suspicious scrutiny of its merit), you were given a signed and dated "hall pass." This was not a mere formality; the hallways were guarded by student "trusties" who checked all hall and restroom passes. If you did not have a class in a given time period, you had to sit in a supervised study hall, and you had to keep absolutely silent therein. Any disruptions (or attempts to communicate with anyone else in the study hall) were dealt with via varying degrees of a well established system of punishments. These included boredom (such as detention after school), being exposed to peer group ridicule, and, in cases of insubordination, corporal punishment.

In the rich kid school, things were night and day different. If you had a class, it was generally recommended that you attend, as that would help you pass the test, but if you didn't feel like going, well, that was your business. If you had no classes (or again, even if you did), you could pretty much do what you felt like doing. For example, if you felt like getting some fresh air, you could hike the nature trails on the beautifully landscaped grounds. If it was too cold to go outside, you could maybe go shoot some hoops in the gym. Throughout the building there were lounges and various "common areas" with plush seating where you could hang out with other students. If you sought quiet and solitude, the library was the best choice, and by the way, if you wanted to take out a book, you just helped yourself, and you returned it whenever you felt like it.

There were no "trustie" hall monitors, there were no bars on the windows, and, unlike the poor kid public schools of that era, no corporal punishment. Actually, there weren't any punishments, period, as there were so few rules to break in the first place that the very thought was somewhat ludicrous. The only punishment, if you can call it that, was other people telling you that you had hurt them by not honoring the precious trust they had placed in you.

So just to repeat the point: in the poor kid school, there was little or no trust. In the rich kid school, there was an overabundance of it.

In case you haven't made the connection yet, one of the biggest reasons why poor kids are poor and rich kids are rich is this: it's because poor kids have no trust, while rich kids have massive amounts of it. And trust, not money, is the basis of wealth.

Trust is key to making the whole monetary system work. Every check you write requires trust on the part of the person taking it. When buying a car or a house, if no one trusted anyone else, we would all have to pay in cash. This of course assumes that the seller is willing to trust that your paper money is worth something, otherwise you'd have to barter with goats. And every time you use a credit card, your wealth of having that convenience, along with your having that instant access to a line of credit, relies entirely upon the credit card company trusting you to pay your bill. The cash in your pocket only has value because we collectively trust the Federal Reserve to maintain its value. Without our collective trust, it's just paper. Without trust, there is no money. So without trust, it is pretty much impossible to build and maintain wealth.

To see how the emotions of trust overwhelmingly affect money and wealth, well, consider the recent screw-ups on Wall Street. When people talk about "the great recession," many people try to define it in purely mathematical terms, of there being "a loss of two trillion dollars" in the stock market.

This is mechanical thinking and has nothing to do with the root cause. The stock market did not "lose" two trillion dollars in 2008. It's not like someone put two trillion dollar bills in his pants pocket and accidentally ran it through the wash. What happened was, many people who had trusted the stock market stopped trusting it, and once that fragile sense of trust was gone, no one was willing to risk buying anything. Without trust, even the banks cannot do business with other banks.

So the money didn't just disappear. In fact, we're not even talking about cash money here; we're talking about presumptions of the "market" being a trustworthy place. Nothing tangible got hauled out the door. If you look around, you will see that the desire for products and services is still out there, the manufacturing capacity is still out there, the labor force is still out there, the natural resources are still out there, and the money supply itself is still out there. What *was* lost, and what we are still trying to rebuild, is the trust that is necessary to link it all together. Money does not go where there is no trust. And poor kids have very little trust to work with.

The rich kids in the rich kid school were wealthy, but not by simply "having money." The cash was just a downstream result. Upstream, they had trust. They had wealth in terms of having people in their lives that they could depend upon, and this gave them the wealth of confidence. They were also rich in the freedom that came from being trustworthy themselves. They were completely trusted to not burn down the school or get into knife fights at recess, hence they were given much greater freedom of movement. They were trusted to pass their exams, so they were free to study when they felt like it.

The poor kids were not trusted, hence they had very little freedom.

If no one trusts you to honor their needs and desires, then they will give you as little trust, and by extension, as little money, as possible. The more trust you command, the more money you have. Warren Buffet is rich because people trust him to safeguard and grow their money. The fact that they trust him creates desire to invest, and money is just a number ascribed to that desire. No trust = no desire. No desire = no money. Therefore, No trust = no money.

A big part of wealth is having other people do stuff for you, and how can you use other people's services if you don't trust them to do a good job? When trust is absent, you end up sending them all home and doing it all yourself. When a lack of trust makes you stop exchanging goods and services, the result is poverty. It is the same as subsistence farming. If you have cash but you can't trust anyone to honor a contract, your money becomes worthless.

The trouble with being a poor kid is, if you have grown up in a world without trust, how do you acquire it? Since one of the three primary beliefs of poor kid thinking is that the universe is a negative place, how can you even begin to trust anyone? To a poor kid, trust is totally foreign. They have never seen it, much less experienced it.

When you are a poor kid, you are usually surrounded by other poor kids and poor adults who are immersed in poor kid thinking as well. This means everyone is assuming universal negativity. This negativity applies to how they perceive everything, including you, so they will just assume that, like everyone else around here, you are careless, irresponsible, a crook, or worse. You may never even get a chance to prove you are trustworthy (and even if you do, they still might not believe it). And you may have had your own trust violated, so from that you learned to not trust anyone either.

After all that experience in a non-trust environment, you simply may not any idea of how to behave as a trustworthy person. Handling responsibility – both getting it and giving it – takes practice.

For poor kids, trust illiteracy is a huge problem. Some poor kids learn to trust no one. Others are so desperate to change their circumstances that they will trust *anyone*. In that case, their lack of experience in managing trust makes them easy marks for con artists.

Then there is the reverse, i.e., resistance to letting anyone trust you. Many poor kids have difficulty in letting others trust them, partly because they don't even trust themselves, and also because they are not sure of the extent of the implied responsibilities that will come with being trusted. Self-confidence is trust in your self, and if you lack trust, you lack confidence. Getting that big promotion may mean handling way more mutual trust than you are used to, giving you motivation to just stay where you are.

Some poor kids go the opposite extreme and take on too much trust, in the form of too much debt or other promises they cannot keep; when disaster inevitably strikes, despite the best of intentions, they become untrustworthy in the eyes of others, and again, poverty ensues from the lack of trust.

Rich kids grow up in an environment where trust is commonplace, hence they learn how to handle it. They have people to trust, and so they have a reference and a backstop when they encounter people they do not trust. Poor kids don't have this.

Since poor kids are constantly exposed to lack and/or violation of trust, they must somehow adapt in order to survive.

A common poor-kid thinking adaptation is to think that it is a sign of cleverness to never trust anyone. One can easily come to believe that one is "smarter" for never trusting anyone and keeping one's money in a mattress. In an environment where you cannot trust most people, this is a reasonable and sensible response. (This gets reinforced via a psychic reward, i.e., a delicious feeling of relative moral superiority to all the seemingly untrustworthy people around you.) This blanket mistrust may seem like a sound policy, but in reality, it is poor kid thinking. Over the long haul, it is disaster. True, you may be avoiding a few potential bad results, but then again, you're never going to build anything positive either.

If you are a poor kid, along with all the other stuff you didn't get, you didn't get the benefits of trust training.

Rebuilding your trust in yourself, and moving towards living in a world where other people trust you and you trust other people, is a major step in going from being a poor kid to being a rich kid.

9

Poor Kids, Rich Kids, and Negotiations

Before delving further into specific emotional elements of poor kid thinking, let us first consider a purely practical element of converting you from a poor kid to a rich kid. This has to do with . . . *negotiations*.

Just about every time money changes hands in a major way, it is preceded by a discussion of what the price will be. Generally speaking, the seller's asking price is high and the buyer's first offer is low. What happens after that, who knows. As you will soon see, poor kids are generally hobbled when it comes to negotiations, and inevitably get a lousy deal. Hopefully, we can now get you to think and negotiate more like a rich kid.

To start us off, if you can stand the thought of going back one more time to that screaming kid in the checkout line, well, bear in mind that the screaming you heard was the sound of someone who was not having a very good negotiation experience. And when that poor kid grew up, especially if that poor kid was you, right from the get-go your confidence was not very high, given your previous track record in getting what you wanted by negotiating. The pain of that past refusal experience lurks in the subconscious, and the mere thought of revisiting that psychic pain is enough to make anyone run for the exit.

You would rather not do any negotiating at all ever again, thank you very much.

But now, as an adult, to get what you want, you have to sit down across the table from some stranger and again face this dark nightmare. You are about to ask for a candy bar again, in the form of asking someone else to pay you money or do something for you. Your past experience in such matters has conditioned you to assume that it will not go well. This presumption of *universal negativity* is a tremendous disadvantage in the realm of negotiations. So, let's calmly and carefully examine the whole process and see if we can't make some improvements.

The first disadvantage is the simple lack of knowledge and experience. There are many standard "negotiation techniques," and since most poor kids don't have much to trade in the first place, they never have occasion to learn them. The second disadvantage for poor kids is that they have been taught to put more trust in outside authority than in themselves, making them vulnerable to manipulative people. But perhaps the biggest problem for poor kids in negotiations is just the gut feeling of dread when negotiations occur, as there is an automatic expectation of a bad result.

Poor kid thinking always assumes that the world is a negative adversarial place, where everyone fights with everyone else over scarce resources. In a world of limited resources, it also assumes that there must be a winner and a loser of every negotiation. Poor kid thinking also preaches that you have to be just as nasty and negative in response to this negative world in order to effectively deal with it. If you don't wish to be evil and negative, so the theory goes, then your only choice is to submit and surrender, and be satisfied with a feeling of moral superiority and not much else.

This is poor kid thinking, and like all poor kid thinking, it is simply not true. A negotiation does not have to be a negative experience for anyone. Sometimes a negotiation is just a calm discussion and clarification between well meaning people of just who wants what. The poor kid presumption that one must be shrewd or tough in negotiations only applies to some negotiations, not all. It is far better to be calm than tough, and it's far better to simply be clear on what you want and how much you want it, than to be some sort of sadistic manipulative game player. To always see negotiations as negative adversarial situations is a symptom of poor kid thinking.

So to begin rethinking your poor kid negotiating skills, let's consider the basic elements of a standard, relatively unemotional, healthy, non-poor-kid-thinking negotiation. Just to give you an example, let's say Jack and Jill are negotiating a fee for Jack, for mowing Jill's lawn.

Jack says, "I'll do it for $100." Jill refuses this offer. She says, "No, you can't have $100. I'll give you $10." Jack refuses her offer and then makes a counter offer, maybe $90, which Jill refuses, and then Jill makes another counter counter offer, maybe $20, which is also refused. Hopefully, they eventually get to something like a price of $50, and they both agree. If so, they both got what they wanted, but *only* after both of them had been repeatedly told they could *not* have what they just asked for.

That is, of course, how rich kids negotiate. For a poor kid, right off the bat, there are several problems:

1) As you now know, in a poor kid thinking world, desire is bad. Therefore, in negotiations, a huge disadvantage for poor kids is the sense of sin, i.e., the sense that they are doing something wrong by simply expressing desire. This gut feeling clouds all calm logic. It's all one can do to make the first ask, much less quickly recover from a refusal experience and make another "ask," risking yet another unbearable refusal experience.

2) Next, the memories of past checkout-counter refusals are so terrible that a poor kid may seek to avoid them at all costs. To do this, a common approach is to simply set the initial offer at such a ridiculously low or high level that it will be immediately and eagerly accepted without any other bargaining. The poor kid's biggest desire– of avoiding being reminded of any past "refusal" trauma– may be greater than any desire for more money.

3) Next there is the problem with "universal limitation" thinking. Limitation thinking creates desperation. For example, you may be so broke, and without any financial "cushion," that you believe that you cannot refuse any offer, as you cannot risk the other person giving up and not coming back with a counter offer.

4) Next, poor kids are taught to not expect very much, and just generally believe that there isn't very much to have, period. So poor kids end up simply not asking for very much. This is not because they think they don't deserve it;

it's because they simply don't think anyone has the money to pay them, so there is no point in asking, and

5) Again, due to a belief in universal limitation, you may fear that by demanding more money, you are causing the other party some extreme hardship. You may fear that they may be in worse straits than you. (Do you recall the 3-kid, 2-drumstick dilemma, of always creating pain in others by getting what you want?) If so, your conscience may prevent you from asking for an appropriate fee for your services. You may feel obliged to accept as little as possible so as to not cause hardship to others. Or if you do bring yourself to demand more money, you end up hating yourself, for having been so selfish and cruel to someone else in doing so. Again, poor kid thinking always leads to adversarial, negative, scarcity-driven energy. The real profit in business is to be found in long term relationships, and it is impossible to maintain healthy long-term business relationship if this kind of negative experience constantly occurs.

Now another problem in negotiations has to do with more personal issues. Poor kids live a world where desire is bad, and that includes the desire for them . . . as people. A job is more than money. It is also a treasure trove of belonging and social status. So if you were a true poor kid (in the sense that love and acceptance were scarce, and no one gave you basic social acceptance), you may have a desperate need for a potential employer to fill that emotional void. You may desperately want, along with money, the feeling of belonging that comes with having a job. So in negotiations, you have yet another handicap, in that you are overly eager to consummate the deal. You want some kind of reward other than the money, and so you may take less money in order to assure that you get the "psychic income," i.e., a sense of connection, belonging, and social status, that you currently lack.

But for all of these other problems, again, the real problem for poor kids is that a negotiation is always a series of potential refusal experiences; and for a poor kid, refusals are hard. This is because refusal experiences are what caused the pain and trauma that created poor kid thinking in the first place.

Now of course, rich kids have all had refusal experiences too, but not the way poor kids do. Rich kids are refused some things, but they are also generally given what they really need. Poor kids, on the other hand, can remember asking for something really important . . . like say, a blanket on a cold night . . . and not getting it. This kind of refusal experience is a whole lot different than not getting something like, say, a toy fire truck. You can forget about the fire truck, but a whole night (or a whole winter) of shivering is not so easily overlooked. So for poor kids, refusal experiences are a much more difficult and painful memory. So let's see if we can't go back in on the patient and fix some of this.

To start, a big part of going from being a poor kid to being a rich kid is to now do several things that you were once repeatedly and harshly taught not to do. The first of these is expressing desire. Easier said than done, but just remember, the people who taught you that "desire was bad" were lying to you. It can't be stated any more plainly than that. It just isn't true. You can't always get what you want, but it's okay to want, and it's okay to politely (and if necessary, firmly) express your want.

Next, it is essential to understand that, to negotiate like a rich kid, there is nothing evil or sinful about politely putting another person through a series of refusal experiences. And you must accept that you may have to go through a few of them yourself. The trick is very simple: just don't let your mind associate the refusals of today with the refusals of yesteryear. They are completely separate. This can be hard but it is doable, and is done mostly by just not thinking.

Your training in universal limitation may come into play. In a world of presumed limited everything, poor kids are always dogged by the fear that this job or this house may be "the last one.'" Many salespeople prey on this common vulnerability in order to quickly move merchandise. When you get the first offer, you may panic and take it because you will think it is the "only offer."

You may also have remnants of concern (or guilt) for your little brother or sister going without a chicken leg drumstick, and so you may become overly concerned about the other person's point of view, to the point where you buy something you don't need out of concern for their welfare. This is a wonderfully good intention gone terribly awry. Also it may be evidence of a bit of an ego problem; do you think you are responsible for everyone else? You aren't. You can't play a game and be the referee at the same time. Other people need to hold up their end. They have the same access to the infinite resources of the universe that you do. If they claim to be pathetic, well, here's their chance to discover strength they didn't know they had.

Next, remind yourself of this simple fact: You now have permission to say "no." You can put other people through the unspeakable pain of a refusal experience. If you cannot bring yourself to say "no" to anyone, you need to get someone else to do your negotiating for you, because negotiating is all about saying "no." They call it "negotiating" for a good reason: it's all negative. If it was all about saying yes, it would be called "pos-otiating."

Children of scarcity tend to fall into one of two groups: either they put everyone else through constant refusal experiences, or they can't bear to put *anyone* through a refusal experience. If you are the latter, be aware, this is a major handicap in your business life. Many people will take advantage of your aversion to saying "no."

Now of course you shouldn't necessarily start saying no all the time and refuse every first offer. For one thing, there are lots of other poverty thinkers out there besides yourself. They don't like to negotiate either, so they put their "best price" on the table at the start. That way they only have to go through one refusal with you before going on to the next. But in that case, if you ask for more and are refused, if you keep your mouth moving you can usually back up and accept the original offer. Expressing desire is okay. It is also okay for others to say no. The idea here is to free up the expression of desire and be more accepting of the "rich kid" free flow of acceptance and refusal. Refusals are not as hard or as permanent once you leave a poor kid thinking world. In a rich kid world, there is always a second option if the first one doesn't work out.

Remember, in a negotiation it is not just *your* want that is being addressed. Someone else is getting their wants met as well. It is a team effort. Poor kids have a need to control negotiations, because to them it is a dangerous situation. They often try to "control" the situation by giving up way too much. This is, again, because of an ingrained habit of trying to always avoid refusals, as well as the habit of keeping any expression of want at a bare minimum.

If you think desire is bad, then you will think that the customer's desire you are getting paid to meet is bad too, hence you should not be working at all. So, think of other people's desire as a good thing. And remember that your getting paid for meeting their desire is a good thing as well.

If you enter into negotiations with these concepts in mind, you will be able to calmly refuse the first, second, or even the final offer, because you know that there is an infinite number of future offers to come from other opportunities. Of course, use your head and be practical. If it's the right offer for you and it's a fair offer for all concerned, go for it. And if it's not a perfect deal (they seldom are), well, at least you will have more than you did before.

*   *   *

At this point it is time to introduce a common variable in negotiations, which is, the kind of person you are negotiating with.

You may be dealing with a wealth-minded person, or you may be dealing with a poverty-minded person. After all, poor kid thinking is rather widespread, and fixing it in yourself will not necessarily fix it in everyone else. If you are dealing with a poverty thinker, it's hard to win no matter what you do, as they are forever in that awful three-kids-two-chicken-drumsticks-no-one-will-ever-be-happy mode. They will actually do things to re-enact it, on you or on themselves. What you may discover with such people is that sometimes the other person does not really want your goods or services very much. Instead, they believe desire is bad, so by making unreasonable demands, they seek a justification for not letting themselves have the benefit of your services. (Of course, when you finally get pushed to your limit and say no, they tell you what an awful rude selfish mean person you are.) Or, they may take a different tack and challenge *your* desire . . . . for adequate payment. Poverty minded people are constantly reducing value (and by extension, desire), both of themselves and of others (if they can). This is shown by their always trying to pay less for anything and everything. They believe they only have permission to spend minuscule amounts, so they are eager for cheap goods and services, even though over the long haul it is generally better to invest in higher quality. They drag down the quality of life for everyone. Their loyalty to the idea that "desire is bad" makes them constantly look for flaws and other reasons to not want anything and not pay for anything. They take great joy in useless free stuff, not because they need it, but because they "won" by getting something for themselves while someone else got nothing in return. To them, this feels like home.

Worse, if they are a child of scarcity, they may want to pass their trauma on to others, and so they will actively shame (and thereby lessen) your energy of desire. They see their own desire as evil, so they may only be interested in your product if there is no desire for it, i.e., if it is free. Such people see themselves as being undesirable, and they want to see if they can make you feel the same way and help them rationalize their sorry state of being. So be it. If they are not willing to participate in a mutually fair exchange of value, you should not do business with them. To be a successful negotiator, one must think like a rich kid, and rich kids know there is plenty more stuff out there if this item isn't exactly what you wanted. Therefore rich kids have the option to just walk away and wait for the better offer which will inevitably come. Poor kids have a hard time seeing beyond the horizon, due to the "universal limitation" aspect of poor kid thinking. Rich kids know there will always be another item, and there will always be another opportunity to make a deal.

Now if you encounter poor-kid-thinking people in a negotiation, they may try to take advantage of your own poor kid thinking and use it against you. They may "cry poor" and make you feel guilty for asking for so much, and thus make you feel you are somehow impoverishing them by asking for a fair price. This can be very hard to take, as it brings up your own three-kids-two-chicken-drumsticks trauma. But one simple fix is, instead of worrying about how you may be causing them privation by making them come up with some cash, do them a favor: The only way they are ever going to become empowered in this money-speaking world is if they learn their own value. And a great way for that to happen is for you to present them with a good example to follow. Stand up and see yourself as having value, and demand a fair price for yourself. Yes, this is "tough love," but it is still love. And loving yourself is a big part of being a rich kid.

10

Resentment vs. Optimism

Our poor kid hero once had occasion to go and spend an afternoon with some rich kids, in a rich kid home, on Christmas Day.

Now bear in mind, up to this point this poor kid had only seen Christmas in his own house. For him, Christmas had always been a rather difficult affair. His parents always lacked enough money to buy very many presents. Even in a good year, they were only able to give him and his siblings maybe two or three gifts to open on Christmas morning. A feeling of disappointment was common. So, the events that transpired before him in this rich kid house were nothing short of amazing.

There were three small children in this rich kid house. The standard early-morning gift-opening extravaganza had already taken place. But then, in the middle of the afternoon, the grandparents drove up in their Mercedes-Benz station wagon. It was loaded to the rafters with dozens of gifts for each of these three little kids.

It took several loads of boxes and bags to get all these gifts into the house, and immediately, these three kids tore into them like little Tasmanian devils. At least, they did at first. You see, there were SO MANY gifts for these kids that, after a while, they developed what could best be called "unwrap fatigue." Like tourists trying to see the entire Louvre Museum in one day, the sheer volume of gifts had literally overwhelmed their perceptual capacity. Their little eyes started to glaze over, and their little hands were getting carpal tunnel syndrome. Their mother eventually had to step in. She called a halt to the proceeding, and put the remainder of the unwrapped gifts away for opening at a later date.

To this poor kid who was observing all this, these events were, in a word, shocking. He had never been exposed to real life opulence before.

So what do we take from this? Well . . .

There are many things lacking in a poor kid's life, but there is one thing that there is always plenty of, and that is . . . resentment. For poor kids, the default standard procedure is for you to just go without, period. Getting your basic needs met is a constant struggle. You usually have to pull and push and kick and knock, until your demands are finally met.

Even when you do finally get something you want, it's nowhere near the amount of stuff you were hoping for (and it certainly can't make up for the backlog of stuff you haven't gotten up 'til now). And of course you must always be bracing yourself for the battle to get your basic needs met on the morrow. Thus, poor kids live in a world of constant and ever-growing resentment.

Resentment is like a cancerous growth. It starts with the initial resentment felt towards the people that are seemingly withholding the things that you need. Then there is resentment for your being made to feel guilty for wanting anything in the first place. Then there is the resentment you inevitably feel towards the rich kids you observe, who always look like they are getting so much more than you. And then there is the resentment . . . for always being made to feel resentment. It is a truly vicious cycle.

The above mentioned three little rich kid girls had a very different emotional orientation regarding resources coming to them. One is tempted to say they felt gratitude, but that isn't really it. Overall, this poor kid did not observe a great deal of gratitude being overtly expressed by the rich kids. It's not that they were ungrateful; they just didn't have occasion to go through that big emotional swing from "not having" to "having" that usually induces overt expressions of gratitude. But the lack of gratitude was not the big issue. To this poor kid, what was so striking about these rich kids was the *total lack of resentment*. In its place, they had a calm optimism.

These three little rich kids lived in an environment where a general feeling of positive expectation was allowed to naturally develop, and resentment was not allowed to take root.

Resentment energy is the exact polar opposite of optimism energy, and the two cannot exist in the same space. To be a rich kid, one must remove resentment, and instead cultivate a feeling of calm optimistic expectations.

One might argue that resentment is not an expectation. One might assume that it only arrives after a bad experience. But emotional energy has little respect for the time-space continuum; resentment energy will fly ahead of you, perpetuating the scarcity experiences that keep it alive. If you are resentful here and now, that will pollute all your expectations of what will happen tomorrow. Your emotional resonance will invite events that will support that resentment result, and you will be resistant to positive events that a sense of optimistic expectation will invite.

The resentment you cultivated as a child was actually created to distract you from your own sadness over the injustice you were experiencing. It was the only fix you had at the time, so you may have become fond of it. It's time to clean house. Resentment, like so many elements of poor kid thinking, is not an energy per se so much as it is a method of blocking your energy of feeling, thus serving as an emotional anesthetic. Remember, money and emotion are the same thing, and if you are blocking your emotions to kill the pain of not getting things, you are also blocking the energy that will bring money to you. You have to think hard, deeply, and with high velocity of emotional flow about good things, and yes, this will open you to the painful things of the past, but take the pain you must if you are to heal it. If you focus solely on bad things in order to numb yourself, you will be lost to poor kid thinking forever.

You can live without resentment. Facing and processing the sadness/ injustice that caused it is hard, but it is an essential part of moving from being a poor kid to a rich kid. Also, remember this: once you make the transition, you'll be an even richer kid. This is because your enjoyment of the things you have will be that much greater. Unlike the never-been-poor rich kids, you'll appreciate what you have, because you will remember what it felt like to go without.

Okay, now that we have dealt with the opposing energies of resentment and optimism, here is a lab activity to help you get rid of resentment.

Here is your assignment: On a sheet of paper or on your electronic device, make a list. This list should include all of the very best things that have ever happened to you. This can be your first love, your current significant other, the appearance in your life of your best friend (feel free to list a subset of favorite things you have done with them), a fabulous trip abroad, or some out-of-the blue "mitzvah" someone once did for you long ago.

If you don't have a laundry list of fabulous trips abroad, best friends, or past lovers, don't despair. If you feel your list is running short, bear in mind as you read this that merely having the eyesight to read this is pretty cool, especially when compared to those who have lost their vision. And if you are not currently experiencing chronic pain, there are many people who feel intense envy of you.

Once you have made this list, take a minute or two to just sit and read through it once or twice every day, and just let these thoughts take you away to a pleasant reverie. In fact, any time you have an unpleasant interaction, and you feel yourself going into a state of resentment, see if you can distract yourself from any negative thoughts by reading and pondering this list.

Now at this point we should point out that this is a potentially very powerful exercise. Again, optimism and resentment are mutually exclusive emotional energies. You can't feel both of them at the same time. Poor kids tend to be mired in resentment. They are certainly justified in doing so, but negative thoughts are seeds that yield negative results. Resentment is not going to lead to your being a rich kid.

Wealth is, as much as anything else, a state of positive consciousness. Reading this customized list of your personal wealth of experience will put you in a state of feeling "rich." After all, if you had all the money in the world, the feelings inspired by thoughts of this list are what you would seek to acquire with it. Unlike envisioning piles of money or "future wealth," this is envisioning actual "wealth experiences" . . . ones that you have already achieved.

Now here is the catch: When you put this list down, your positive state of mind will now stand in stark contrast to any poverty consciousness. It's a little like painting a room in an old house; it will suddenly make you realize how drab and dingy the rest of the place is. You will become much more aware of the "poor kid thinking" elements that are lurking in your mind. You will then be forced to consciously choose between the two polarities; for example, feeling anger towards the people who have underpaid you vs. appreciation for those who have overpaid you.

With this greater consciousness will come greater awareness of unpleasant things, but then, with that greater awareness, there also comes greater motivation to take positive action to fix them.

Eventually, you can take this exercise to the next level and simply not let yourself have any resentment in the first place. At that point, you will no longer need to do the "work" of counteracting your resentment with a positive memory, since there will be no resentment to counteract in the first place. This simple idea of achieving the effortless state of "non-resentment" is key to converting yourself from a poor kid to a rich kid.

Be advised, however, that when you change your overall emotional resonance in this manner, this will make you very aware of the resentment energy residing in other people that used to seem normal to you. Addressing resentment can be very disruptive. Please use caution and proceed at your own risk.

11

Compensation vs. Reward

For the average poor kid, one of the most convoluted ways of looking at money is seeing it, not as a byproduct of a pleasant interaction, not as a reward, not as a symbol of intrinsic value, nor an expression of gratitude, but seeing it as a sort of lame apology. It is easy for a poor kid to see money as "barely adequate compensation" for doing something unpleasant.

This is a common outgrowth of the poor kid expectation that life is a zero sum game. In a poverty world, if someone gets a chicken drumstick, someone else always goes without. In terms of money as "compensation," the good/bad equal balance is achieved in another way: in order to get something good (cash), one must also go through something bad (unpleasant work). The idea that you could get paid for something you enjoy is foreign to poor kids. The idea that you could have a purely positive experience, and not have it zeroed out by an equal negative experience, does not exist in a poor kid thinking world. Universal-limitation-based poor kid math says that something bad always has to happen in order for something good to happen, and vice versa, to keep things nice and finite/limited.

One of the worst ways you can approach money is to see it as a scarce commodity that will only be begrudgingly given to you in exchange for doing something you don't want to do. When you are "compensated" for your work, well, thank goodness there are people who are willing to dig ditches in exchange for money, but this is an inherently limiting approach to acquiring wealth. It is viewing both yourself and your own "value," and the value of money, in a purely physical / mechanical dimension. It is based on the learned poor kid presumption that the world is a negative place. It assumes that the world seeks to keep money from you by default. It assumes you can only get money if you are willing to exchange something precious for it, like your health, your sense of well being, or maybe your self respect. In a poor kid world of presumed universal limitation, life is always a zero sum game, so whatever pleasure the money may give you, it is instantly cancelled out by the pain of what you had to do to get it.

For rich kids, they learn something completely different. One of the things most noticeable about truly wealthy people is just how much they love the "work" they do. Along with the cash, they also get fulfillment and prestige.

If you make your money by doing work that you don't enjoy, no matter how eager or greedy you are, you will necessarily run into all sorts of obstacles and limitations. For example, no matter how much ambition you have to "make money," you will eventually run out of the "will power" necessary to get yourself out of bed and go do something all day that you don't like to do. You can only convince yourself that the unpleasant work is "worth the money" for just so long, until you finally decide it is not worth any amount of money to keep doing this lousy job that you hate so much. You never really had a chance to create any real wealth, because the more money you made, the more unhappy you became by doing ever more unpleasant work.

If your work provides no thrill, if it excites no passion, if it does not offer any sense of intrinsic reward of personal pleasure or fulfillment just from the doing of it, then the only reward for your work is the cash. That must then be converted into "reward" by spending it on something else, done by someone else, for you. But of course, you will hesitate to spend the money, because it was so unpleasant to acquire it; spending it means you must go back to doing the something you do not like in order to replace what you spent, so spending it always creates a conflict of desires. (There's that "desire" word again.)

If the work by itself does not have its own intrinsic joy reward for you, then the money is all there is. That means that all of your real enjoyment of life, if any, exists outside of your work life. Are there that many hours in a day to "spend" that you can attain adequate "compensation" for the time you used up working at something you don't enjoy doing?

If, on the other hand, you think like a rich kid and brazenly allow two positives to occur, i.e., you get paid for doing something you enjoy, well, even if you are getting paid by the hour, your potential for financial gain becomes virtually unlimited, because you end up working 10, 12, 15 hours a day just because you like doing it. When you enjoy your work, you essentially double your reward, because you're getting paid AND you're having fun while doing it. And if your work provides meaningful help to others, that is essentially a third level of reward, so now you have tripled the reward you are obtaining from the work you do.

And when you work at something for a long time just out of the joy of it, you will of course inevitably get better and better at it. And when people experience your commitment and passion, pretty soon word starts to get out. You establish "brand" that creates ever more desire for your services, hence more value is added to what you do and what you offer.

And then if you want to be a really rich kid, you should transcend the idea of work-for-pay altogether and instead think about work solely as a subset of *purpose*.

When you have a big dream and a big goal, now you are opening the floodgates, allowing people to join you and support you in that effort. No matter what your purpose in life was this morning, it was probably too small. Don't think in just physical terms of a big result, for even big results are limited. Instead, think in terms of "big intentions." If they are big enough, you will probably never fully realize them, but people will get excited and support you if you dare to make the attempt. Being humble and willing to accept just enough to get by is not something anyone wants to contribute to. Such limited poor kid thinking is an insult to the divinity within you and everyone else. Think like a rich kid. Think big.

12

Getting the Most for the Most

At the poor kid school, students were required to do assignments that were consistently dull. There was a common excuse made for this. There was a presumption that these poor kids weren't very bright, and so the only way to pound anything into their dull little poor kid brains (and they must be dumb if they are poor, right?) was by endless repetition, sort of like how you would train a dog.

There was tremendous emphasis placed on doing this dull work over and over again with as few errors as possible. Everyone was "graded" in terms of how well they conformed to a given rubric, i.e., a single generic standard of performance.

Because the work was so dull and uninspiring, the kids all lost focus in short order. This meant it was like pulling teeth for the teachers to get the kids to learn anything at all. In this vicious cycle of lost interest / presumption that the kids were slow / more boring repetition that led to loss of interest, the homework and tests were essentially made "easy enough" so most of the kids would pass even though they were not really engaged in the subject matter. Poor kid thinking is always about less of everything, and in a poor kid school, this meant less interest, less information, and less work. Again, in poor kid thinking, desire is bad, and so the desire to learn and better oneself was also bad as well. Since the poor kid school work was so unpleasant due to its being so dull, it was a constant game to see how one could get the best grade for the least amount of unpleasant time and effort spent on it.[1]

In the rich kid school, that all went out the window. You would think that these spoiled rotten rich kids would get pampered and have an easy ride. Not so. The rich kid school was about more, more, more. More work, more information, more study, more intensity. It was extremely challenging. The work was hard, but it was not hard in the sense of being hard to take because of boredom. It was hard in a good way. Instead of being about getting the most reward you could get for the smallest amount of effort, it was how to get the most . . . for the biggest amount of effort.

At the rich kid school, the teachers piled on massive amounts of homework. The classes were challenging. One was constantly being urged to max out one's schedule and take on individual projects that were going to take enormous amounts of time and energy. Yes, it was more work, but the fun and excitement of it fed the energy and thus made it possible. Yes, it was "more work," but it engaged all those joyful endorphins of problem solving.

---

1   . The idea of allowing them to do something truly challenging never occurs to anyone, as they do so poorly on the boring simple stuff. It never occurs to anyone that they are bored and unfocused because the work is so simple and easy.

From a poor kid perspective, these rich kids were all suckers. To a poor kid, work of any kind is expected to be dull and unpleasant, and one is never paid much anyway, so why would you do more work than absolutely necessary? This minimal approach to everything is a key element of poor kid thinking.

Of course, the less work you do, the less money you tend to make. Poor kids tend to think in terms of inverse ratios, i.e., that victory is somehow attained by getting a lot for doing the least. Rich kids don't accept this upside down logic. They do a lot, and they expect a lot, and of course . . . they get a lot.

13

Brand Names vs. Generics

One of the biggest differences between a poor kid school and a rich kid school has to do with uniformity.

In the poor kid public school, there was a general policy of uniformity. This allowed the management to achieve economies of scale, similar to how one approaches manufacturing. For example, the textbooks were often the same throughout an entire state, and had a typical "shelf life" of ten years or so. That meant an entire generation of all the poor kids (in all the poor kid schools across the state) studied from the same small handful of textbooks. And in turn, that meant that even if you studied hard and learned everything in those books, there was still nothing special about your knowledge or your skills. They were exactly the same as everyone else's.

In the rich kid school, individual teachers selected whatever textbooks they deemed appropriate, and the rich kids would then buy their own brand new copies of the latest editions. Price was no object, so the rich kid school textbooks were, if not better, at least not likely to be the same as everyone else's.

In the poor kid school, any kid who excelled academically was of course a geek and had to accept the penalties of being a social misfit. Poor kids who wished to fit in knew they had to bow to peer group pressure, and not excel academically. In the rich kid school, the really smart kids were admired.

We all know the power of peer pressure. And in the overly large classes in the poor kid school, teachers were not above any technique that would help to maintain order, and that included the threat of making someone the object of peer group ridicule if they got "out of line." In other words, in a standard poor kid school environment, there is tremendous pressure from all sides to obey, both from authority figures and from one's peer group. One is taught to conform and be uniform, and there were tremendous psychic penalties for sticking out and being in any way unique.

In the rich kid school, things were again night and day different. Being unique was encouraged. There was a very practical reason for why they encouraged so much individual development. It was collectively understood that "standing out" was *necessary* to getting the biggest traditional goal for a prep-school graduate, which is getting admitted to a top university. To achieve that goal, perfect scores on standardized tests were not enough; one had to show leadership ability and/or other unique attributes in order to stand out and be noticed. And so in a rich kid school, individuality was encouraged, and uniformity was actually discouraged.

These two opposite approaches extend out into life and money management in a rather obvious way: unique rare proprietary items are almost always "worth" far more than commonly available generic commodities. Rich kids are the former, poor kids are the latter.

In the poor kid school, equality and sameness were strictly controlled and enforced. On the most important tests, the word "standardized" was right there at the top in plain letters. The very word means "to cause to conform to a standard." This conformity ultimately leads to one being a commodity item. No matter how good you get at what you do, if you are a generic commodity, your price is tied to the generic commodity marketplace.

No matter how accomplished one becomes at a given generic task, the market will generally only pay you for an adequate job, and so the value of your work is not determined by how good you are, but by how much the market needs that service at a generic level. Poor kids are taught to think of themselves as a member of a category, not as a unique item, and they therefore give up control of their "value" to the commodity marketplace.

One thing that makes it so hard for poor kids to break out of this conformity rut is the "desire for connection" issue: In poor kid culture, one's uniformity becomes the basis of one's sense of belonging. You attain belonging by giving up your claim to a unique identity and spirit.

Rich kids have a much broader spectrum of what is acceptable in terms of personal variations from the norm, and the rich kid school culture allows for much broader possibilities. And when rich kids become "unique" as adults, they can of course charge "one of a kind" proprietary prices for their services– unlike generic poor kids, who, if they have chosen a commodity-worker career path, have relatively little control over what they can charge. The marketplace or the union determines the value of their commodity service, and the fear of being socially excommunicated by their peer group by daring to be unique keeps them from doing any better.

This of course gets us into a whole new realm of "wealth," which is the freedom to simply be yourself. More and more we feel nostalgia for the life of a cowboy or a pioneer settler who owned his own land and was truly independent. We emphasize freedom in all our national symbolism, but real freedom is only available to those who are either homeless, true artists, or very wealthy.

For poor kids, the whole concept of being a unique proprietary item is foreign, confusing, and maybe a little frightening. In poor kid culture, to have desire for anything, even to be yourself, is bad.

In a world where desire is bad, to think of yourself as being "desirable" and worse, to be uniquely desirable, is entirely foreign to a kid steeped in uniformity and non-desire training. For poor kids, they are often not desired as unique individuals, so they seek to be desired indirectly as sources of desirable (if generic) commodity labor. If you are a poor kid, believing that you are a truly unique entity is a tough transition, especially after so many years of being told that your value is determined by how well you conform. But it is key if you want to go from being a poor kid to a rich kid.

14

Rich Kids and Opportunity

There is no question that there will always be a certain amount of unfairness in the world. One of the most blatant elements of "unfairness" when it comes to poor kids vs. rich kids is the whole area of opportunity. Generally speaking, rich kids do not rise "thru the ranks"– they go right to the top. To many, this seems to be immoral. If you expect success to come in an orderly fair-to-all conveyor belt fashion, well of course you will resent anyone who "cuts in line."

Rich kids often get chances for quick success that are simply not available to poor kids. For example, in the rich kid school, there were numerous kids that had trust funds, so, financially speaking, they were already "set for life." And there were other kids whose parents were the owners of large companies. When those rich kids graduated from college, it was pretty much assumed that they would step into these family businesses, in ownership / managerial roles. No starting in the mail room, no climbing through the ranks. They went right to the board room, even though they had no practical experience at all.

For poor kids, of course, such easy opportunities are few and far between. Very few poor kids in the poor kid school were going to inherit much of anything, and it was even less likely that they would get a chance to leap into top management positions. Instead, for those poor kids who had embraced the "American dream," they would set out on a lengthy journey of starting at the bottom and trying to work their way to the top.

Unfortunately, most of the time, they only worked their way to the middle, as that's as far as they got before time ran out, and their dogged linear approach to life was such that they did not belong in a leadership position, where vision, boldness, and non-linear thinking were required.

There is an important lesson to be learned from rich kids in seeking true success, and that is this:

Rich kids don't follow the usual rules.

Rich kids SKIP STEPS. They don't follow the long drawn out standard procedures. They are often thrown, warts and all, with no experience, into a front office, where they just do on-the-job training.

There is a lot to be said for the poor kid approach of going through all the procedures, starting at the bottom, and slowly climbing up the corporate ladder. But while we may decry the rich kids for "cheating" (for taking advantage of a quick and easy opportunity to go right to the top), instead of condemning this, perhaps we should consider just what that means.

Part of poor kid thinking is, again, about limitation and lack of trust and resources, and the lack of resources includes lack of both opportunity and the lack of training for a high paying job. But in any big promotion, and in any truly innovative life-changing strategy, you will always find yourself in situations where you have no idea what you are doing, and perhaps there is no one else in the whole wide world who knows what to do either. After all, when Orville Wright got into the pilot's seat of the world's first airplane, he hadn't taken a single flying lesson. He just took off and did the best he could.

It is easy to resent people who leap into high positions early in life, but maybe we should rethink this. For one thing, these rich kids of these rich families were stinkingly poor in at least one thing, and that was in *having a choice*. Yes, they had a cushy job in the front office waiting for them, but that was the ONLY job waiting for them. Otherwise they would be less than qualified to even fry hamburgers. Poverty does have one advantage, which is the endless number of opportunities to go upwards. Rich kids can only go down.

It is easy to cogitate on the unfairness of rich kids getting big breaks. But if you embrace this kind of disapproval, and you believe it is immoral and unfair for anyone to jump on a chance to leap ahead, well, you may blow it when the heavens open up and give you your big chance to do it too. When your moment comes, you may be cutting in line, you may be jostling the seniority, but if you think maintaining the system is the best way, then you guarantee that you will be waiting the maximum amount of time for your big break. And this assumes that the system will in fact deliver a big break in a nice timely orderly fashion, when in fact this rarely happens.

It is not immoral to act on an opportunity that is yours alone. You are not doing anyone a disservice by grabbing a break that is available only to you. Rich kids know that even for them, big breaks are few and far between, and they are rarely perfect. So they grab them, even though they aren't ready and they know other people may resent their good fortune.

True, when someone does this, they are "breaking the rules" and "being out of uniform." If success to you means never breaking the rules and always fitting in, then that is your happiness, as it is for many people.

Because so many people are hesitant to get out of the line, when fabulous opportunities do appear, it is often hard to find someone who is willing to take them, believe it or not. There is an old saying, "There is always room at the top." Poor kid thinking tends to encourage resentment towards successful people. For poor kids, when they are given a shot at higher success, this creates a hitch step of poor-kid-morality-based hesitation. They look around for permission before acting, and then it's too late. The reason rich kids got rich in the first place was by letting themselves take these rare opportunities to be rich. If you think it is wrong for anyone, yourself included, to grab opportunities to be rich, then you have embraced poor kid thinking.

What is also important to remember is that if you get a big break and step into an unexpectedly high level position, okay, you may not have all the training and skill you wish you had, but the solutions to your problems exist. You will learn the stuff you need to learn. The difference between poor kid thinking and rich kid thinking is that a rich kid figures the information and skill he or she needs will show up in due course. The poor kid, steeped in limitation, thinks that anything that is not in view *now* will never appear. The notion that the heavens will open up and the universe will magically provide needed solutions is a foreign idea to poor kids.

And when you consider the morality of waiting for your turn or grabbing an opportunity that is somewhat specific to you, you should ask yourself this trust question: in your hopes for a better life, are you placing your primary trust in a system outside of yourself, or are you putting your primary trust energy . . . inside yourself? Remember, trust (or the lack thereof) is a major difference between rich kids and poor kids.

So start thinking like a rich kid and have a little faith that what you need will come to you when you need it in some unexpected mystical way. There is no reason why it can't come to you unexpectedly and for no good reason, just like it comes to rich kids.

15

Letting Go

Before we go any further with this process of converting you from a poor kid to a rich kid, there is a bit of a hump that needs to be got over, one that is unfortunately not very pleasant, at least not at first.

The sad fact is, while we tend to talk about "poverty" purely as an arbitrary "line" of a certain number of income dollars being available, living with scarcity is a form of trauma. There are many possible facets of poverty-based trauma. Along with the physical privation, there are the psychological aspects, i.e., the lack of trust, the lack of respect, the lack of safety, the lack of food, and the lack of consistency or predictability. All this hurt may not have been consciously or intentionally done to you. However, that doesn't make it any less of a bruise on your soul.

Like any emotional trauma, the trauma of being a poor kid needs to be grieved and processed. Part of what makes poor kid thinking (or any other destructive behavior, for that matter) get passed on from generation to generation is that facing it and fixing it requires going back into it, and bringing that once purposefully buried fear and pain back up to a conscious level. As long as it remains buried, you must perceive it indirectly with your imagination, and your imagination will make it much larger than it was. You have to face the actual thing to defeat and release it. Yikes.

And what makes it harder or even impossible for some people to face it is this: the poor kid thinking may also be there to protect someone you love, typically someone in your family. The denial and the lies were created to help you maintain your total loyalty to the group, especially to your parents. Acceptance of universal negativity made it "all right" that these people oversaw a poverty experience and did little to stop it. Now, you know that it was not all right. But this is not a blame game. They were just as much victims as you.

So at some point, along with thinking about all these little techniques on a conscious level, give yourself time, if need be, to just sit down and let yourself go into a full fledged crying jag if you feel like it. That kid in the checkout line was in serious pain, and he or she needs to know that an adult (i.e., you) is there for them now to witness and validate their pain, and is now ready and willing to make it safe and all right.

Perhaps the biggest point I wish make to you in this book is this: Money is emotion, and "poor kid thinking" is very much about slowing or stopping the normal flow of emotions in order to cope with the pain of your existence. Here is a new concept for you: It's called "emotional velocity." Letting your emotions flow via tears is one method of increasing emotional velocity. Taking a stick and beating it hard on a rock or some other inanimate object out in the woods while cursing the people who hurt you is another. Giving yourself permission to let your feelings flow is key to opening up the flow of emotion to you via money. The world is filled with opiates, depressants, and soul-numbing violent entertainment. It all feels good (momentarily) because it numbs the pain. But it also numbs everything else. And this opening up of your emotions will make you richer not just in cash, but in your life experience. Unfortunately, for poor kids, this comes at a high cost, of having to "take the pain."

It is beyond the scope of this book to address all the many aspects and methods of recovering from emotional or physical trauma, or just memories of terror. But remember that the experience of going without, especially going without essentials like food, proper clothing, or heat, is not a minor thing. The shame and ridicule of being the poor kid on the bus who wore the same clothes to school every day wasn't much fun either.

Finally, there is an old saying that "living well is the best revenge," but any time you see a negative element like that, watch out, that's the siren song of poor kid thinking. You can't make your life better by making someone else feel envious. You can't fix your past pain by putting the same pain on someone else. Instead, there are these wonderful things in life called accepting, forgiving, and letting go. Sometimes wealth is defined by what you don't have. If you don't have anger or pain, but you do have forgiveness, in at least one dimension you are getting to be more of a rich kid every day.

16

The Poverty of Permission

Along with the many apparently physical and "monetary" barriers to getting what you want, there is another barrier to getting what you want, one that is not physical at all. It's about giving yourself *permission*.

You may finally have the time and the money to take that trip to Paris that you have always dreamed of, but maybe you can't quite bring yourself to just click on the "buy your plane ticket now" button on the airline web site. Some invisible force is making you hesitate. It is not lack of material resources. The issue here is a different kind of scarcity. In this case, it is the scarcity of *permission*.

We all tend to think that this is a free country; therefore, if you are over 21, permission is automatically given, and is always there for any reasonable desire. It isn't. Having the desire, ability, and/or the means to do something does not mean you have the permission to do it.

What is permission? It is a sense that some outside (or inside) authority says it is allowed. It is a vague feeling of *approval*.

Poor kids sometimes never get approval of themselves, or permission to do much of anything. Their very existence may not have ever had approval or permission from any known higher authority. Since they began life as "one more mouth to feed," they can acquire an embedded feeling that they have no permission to be here at all. By extension, the idea that they have permission to use up scarce finite resources for something that is not an emergency is also a foreign, or even sinful, thought.

Poor kids who experience a constant absence of permission tend to rationalize it, they blame it on purely mechanical outside forces that are beyond anyone's control. They tend to think that all the times they did not get permission to do something was because of either a sensible rational decision about proper apportionment of finite resources, or perhaps some other immutable outside physical circumstance. But it is painfully possible that the reason they were not given permission to do something was out of sheer meanness or poverty of spirit. They were told "no" for no real reason other than out of envy, habit, or just a blanket "don't spend any more money than you absolutely have to" policy. It is this culture of automatic denial that is so much a part of scarcity training and poor kid thinking.

For our poor kid hero, when he was in the poor kid school, external permission had to be obtained for just about everything. One had to ask for external permission to use the bathroom or go to the library. If a poor kid student had any kind of original project in mind, they had to get permission to do it from someone on the faculty. The concept of intrinsic permission or "free will" did not exist in that environment. At every moment, one's permission to do anything other than follow orders had to be obtained from someone else, and such permissions were scarce, just as everything else was scarce in a poor kid world. The default was to give you none at all. Of course, as in so many other things, when it came to permission, the rich kid school was night and day different.

As previously stated, at the rich kid school, if you were not in a class, or even if you were supposed to be in one, you were the captain of your fate and master of your soul. You had permission to go do what you wanted. It was a given and a constant. For example, if you had a car, you could skip the usual cafeteria lunch and drive to a local restaurant for some real food, and no, you did not have to "ask permission" to do so.

In the rich kid school, the whole idea of needing external permission was a foreign concept. For rich kids, it was constantly implied that you always had permission to do whatever you wanted to do. The word "permission" implies having consciousness of a higher authority outside yourself to grant it to you, and in the rich kid school, that whole concept was more or less just nonexistent. There were of course certain core requirements, such as minimum credits for graduation, and there was a dress code forbidding the wearing of blue jeans, but other than that, permission was either assumed or just not necessary, or not even thought about in the first place.

The upshot of these differences between the poor kids and rich kids came down to simply this: poor kids have to seek permission from a higher authority to do just about anything, and rich kids already have to ask permission to do just about everything. The rich kids owned the power to give themselves permission, if in fact they ever thought that they had to ask for it in the first place, which they usually did not.

In adult life, this takes a slightly different form. Permission may come from a person in authority, but to a certain extent, when we are adults, money takes the place of hall passes. Money acts as a form of permission, and the lack of money implies a lack of permission. Poor kids go from a lack of institutional permission to a lack of financial permission, i.e., the lack of money. The result is the same. You want to go to the restroom or to Europe, but you are not allowed to go to either, since someone else who has power over you has not given you the hall pass/money/permission.

Poverty is often defined as the lack of money itself and nothing else. It is easy to think that "if we just had some money we would be just like rich people." But money is just an illusion, a reflection of some other emotion. It becomes very hard to tell where the actual lack of money ends and the internal lack of permission, and worse, the lack of trust and the suppression of desire, begins. Since money is so mixed up with the feeling of permission to use it, like the chicken and the egg, for poor kids, it's hard to say which lack came first.

If you want to buy something, if you have the money, you just buy it; there is nothing else to think about. If you want something, but you think it "costs too much," then you do not have permission to buy it. Money represents permission in the mind, and the lack of it acts as a lack of permission. If you do not know how to unilaterally use and handle permission, then you do not know how to use and handle money, and poor kids have little experience with either.

When you are programmed to be a poor kid, you are programmed to think that you will never be rich in permission, because for poor kids, permission is always owned by someone else. You fear having it, for you fear doing something wrong or foolish with it. You fear its unknown exotic power. You have to ask for it to get it, and you may be "granted" some permission, or you may not. The fear of yet another refusal experience makes poor kids hesitant to ask for anything, including permission. Rich kids have no such training, as they have permission–and by extension, cash on hand–all the time. So for them it's just a question of "*what* do I want?" It's never a question of "*will someone else let me have* what I want"?

In observing people who are struggling to seek meaning in their lives, and break from the norm in order to commit to pursuing their heart's true desire, the one thing that interferes with them more than anything else is this confusion about whether or not they are "allowed to do it." Their innate sense of "auto-permit" has somehow been lost. Like the characters in the Wizard of Oz, they become convinced that they must seek out and ask an outside entity to have their fondest wishes granted. For rich kids, this is not a problem; they know they are wearing the ruby slippers. They click their heels all the time, so they don't even bother walking to Oz.

Sadly, you may have cash on hand, but if you were brought up in poor kid mode, you may still not have the sense of permission to use it to do what you want. If so, you may have to spend some of it on an outside coach or consultant just to get a sense of permission to spend it. You end up paying double for everything. That's a good way to remain poor.

Permission and money are very often muddled up and confused in the mind. When we ask our parents for permission to do things, a great deal of the time we are also asking for the money that is necessary to do the thing. And then the confusion starts. The question is, when a refusal comes, what is the cause? Are we being told we cannot have the thing we are asking for because the parents have decided we should not do it for some loving sensible protective reason? Or is the permission/money being withheld for purely dogmatic, poor kid thinking reasons? If the latter, it is always a lie. You are usually told there is some other, more important use for the available finite amount of money. But money is based in emotion and desire, so what is truly lacking? What is lacking, of course, is a free flow of energy. Something, somewhere, is blocked. And poor kid thinking is a form of energy blockage.

As adults, we are constantly being asked to decide what is permissible and what is not– for ourselves and for others. Practical considerations, habits from the past, logic, common sense, and disposable income are all factors in the proceeding, and it is very important to give everything the right label. Otherwise you may think you are "not allowed" to take a trip to Rome just because your parents thought of such things as an extreme extravagance. If you think and feel like a rich kid, you own the ability to give yourself permission, and no one else can withhold it from

you. In fact, you don't even have to think about it, you just
go.

*   *   *

In seeking greater permission, you might want to ask yourself these questions:

Are you really hurting anyone by having a reasonable amount of fun?

Do you fear the resentment of poor people who choose to not give themselves permission?

Does denying yourself something you want result in adding a positive energy to the world?

Does your going without something fun make anyone else any less poor?

If you believe spending money on something fun impoverishes others, have you ever considered that *not* spending your money is impoverishing others . . . for example, airline pilots, and restaurateurs in Rome?

Can life ever be fair to everyone? And is it your job to make life "fair" for other people by going without?

By going without, do you ultimately bring wealth to yourself or to others?

We shall continue the topic of permission in the next chapter, regarding the power of the words "yes" and "no."

17

Yes and No

In many situations, money is simply a piece of paper that says "yes."

Yes, you got the job. Yes, you got the loan. Yes, you can do your research project. Yes, you can buy a house. Yes, you can take that trip.

And the lack of money is a very common way of saying "no." It seems to be at the heart of painful "refusal experiences."

Of course, the money itself doesn't say "yes" or "no." Its presence or absence merely reflects the desire of some human being to say "yes" or "no." That said, these two little words: "yes" and "no" . . . and how they are intertwined with the concept of money, are another instance where rich kids and poor kids are very different.

In the world of poor kids, the word "no" is heard a great deal. "No, you can't have that." "No, that was all there was." "No, you're not good enough to do that."

Sometimes a poor kid won't hear the word "no." Instead, they experience something even worse, i.e., the complete absence of anyone responding to them at all. At least someone saying "no" recognizes one's existence. The absence of "no" means either a) you don't even merit the respect of having your request answered or b) no one heard your request in the first place, meaning you are all alone. In either case, the lack of any response is a low blow to the spirit.

There is a commonly leapt-to conclusion that the reason one is being told "no" is because there is a lack of the needed physical resource, i.e., actual printed dollar bills, to allow one to do this or that. In truth, when people say "there is no money for that," what they are really saying is, "there is no desire to support you in that." (The phrase "There is no money for that" is a handy way for some people to avoid having to openly admit that they simply don't desire to help you. By implying that money is a finite physical resource, and claiming that the "lack" of it is totally beyond their control, this conceals the real "lack, which is a lack of interest in your problems. This lets them pretend to be sympathetic, and maybe even appear to be "fiscally responsible," while they avoid having their own acts of oppression, selfishness, and/or poor kid thinking exposed to scrutiny. Poor kid thinkers, being trained in universal limitation, automatically accept this excuse as plausible.) Again, money is just a number assigned to desire, and if there's "no money" to send you to Europe, that means there's no desire to make the effort that is necessary to send you to Europe. If that desire existed, the money could be found. It might take longer than it does for folks who have ready money in hand, but it can still be acquired eventually *if the desire exists*.

(It is also quite possible that the desire does exist, but it has been successfully suppressed in well-meaning people by a belief in negativity and limitation. The result is the same.)

When a poor kid is faced with the nasty reality that the people they are counting on, who are supposed to love and support him/her, have embraced limitation instead of providing needed support, this is often too painful to bear. Again, the most common poor kid survival response to this situation is to quickly blame the problem on the "power" of this inert theoretical substance called money, and not on the true upstream cause, which is the belief in limitation and/or the suppression of desire on the part of the people involved. In denying the true cause, one starts to think that these pieces of paper have far more power of limitation than they actually do.

Another odd element of the word "no" where poor kids are concerned is, while poor kids hear this word almost constantly, they are never allowed to say it themselves. In other words, poor kids lack yet another thing that rich kids enjoy, which is the option to refuse. Typically, poor kids find themselves in situations where there is no choice, and they have to say "yes" to whatever meager choice has been offered them, because the only other option is to have nothing at all. And worse, sometimes poor kids find themselves in a state of oppression, where they cannot say "no" without risking punishment.

Now you might think that the opposite of a poor kid hearing "no" all the time would be a rich kid hearing "yes" all the time, but that is not the case. In truth, the classic "spoiled rich kid" who always hears the word "yes" and never hears the word "no" is, in many ways, just as impoverished as their poor kid cousins. Real wealth is derived from connection, and having healthy connections with other people requires constant management of emotional boundaries. This includes knowing when to say "yes" and when to say "no," having the permission to say "yes" and "no," and respecting others enough to allow them to say "yes" and "no" to *you*.

When you have a lot of cash lying around, it takes discipline to not take the easy way out, and just give in to every request. It is essential to establish structure and limits. Children may viciously complain about such limits, but they desperately need them in order to feel loved, protected, and safe. Real rich kids live in a world of this constant interconnected negotiating and cultivation of mutual respect.

So for the moment, if you have been a poor kid who never heard the word "yes," the goal is not to put yourself out of balance at the other "spoiled rich kid" end of the spectrum; it's time to put yourself back in balance.

To start, say the word "yes" as often as you can. "Yes, I can have what I want." "Yes, it's a beautiful day filled with endless opportunities." "Yes, other people can have what they want without impoverishing me." "Yes, I'm a worthwhile human being."

And then, oddly enough, start practicing saying "no" as well. It's very important to remember that, as a true rich kid, you have permission to say "no" to the things you *don't* want. "No, I am not going to allow the errors of the past to go on without correcting them." "No, I am not going to conform." "No, I am not going to settle for less than complete fulfillment in life."

Also, when you start to make more money, you may start to find a lot of your old "poor kid" friends and relatives at your door asking for a handout. There is no simple answer to such problems. If they are seeking help in becoming rich kids, okay, but if they just want you to maintain their poor kid lifestyle, if they fail to understand the need to manage capital, you may have to stand your ground and say "no" and risk losing your connection with them. This is perhaps one of the biggest obstacles in converting from a poor kid to a rich kid; you have to leave some poor kids behind that you love very much. Just remember, it was their choice to stay there. If their love for you is conditional on your giving them money or on your remaining poor like them, this is emotional blackmail; this means their love doesn't really exist outside of your eager imagination.

People who imply that you are not allowed to say "no" to them are trying to oppress or impoverish you. As part of getting in touch with your inner rich kid, it is essential that you reacquire your use and control of these two small yet very important words.

18

The Difficulty of Leaving a Poverty System

One of the catch-22's of poor kid thinking is how it affects entire communities of people.

Again, because social connectivity is the #1 desire of most human beings, part of what brings some people together is . . . shared suffering. If everyone in a given group goes without a certain level of monetary advantage, well, that mutual disadvantage becomes a bonding force. So if a single individual within a given social community decides that they want to try and improve their situation, they have two choices: 1) they can attempt to change the attitude and culture of the entire group, so as to have everyone embrace a higher level of material wealth or 2) this person can attempt to get it just for themselves.

Option #1 is awfully difficult, for any number of reasons. Assuming it is even logistically possible, everyone in the group needs to agree that the new system is desirable and attainable, and they all must be willing to make whatever changes and sacrifices are necessary to make this happen. Dogmas are tough enough to change in one person, let alone an entire community, so this seldom occurs unless actual collective survival is threatened. And even then . . .

The second option is to make the improvements on an individual basis. This is of course far more possible, but unfortunately it causes all sorts of problems.

For one thing, if the primary bonding force of a group is a negative, e.g., if it consists of shared privation or collective suffering, then any improvement is a threat to that bonding force. So if one lone individual decides to make a unilateral change so they (individually) no longer have to suffer such privations (for example, if they take a second job, or go to school at night to get promoted, or just suck up to the boss to get a raise), well, their primary "personal connection wealth" . . . i.e., their sense of connection to the group . . . is lost. Their "success" leads to tremendous social failure, as it means they don't fit in any more.

Usually, such people make these personal improvements with the assumption that the group will be happy for them. They assume it will elevate them to ever higher status, but in general, the exact opposite usually occurs. Part of what makes the group's collective suffering tolerable is the belief that there is nothing anyone can do about it. If one lone individual disproves that group dogma, that embarrasses everyone who believes in it. Rather than accept the truth, to maintain group cohesion they will take the easier path of merely saying this person (who has created some greater individual success) did it either by cheating or by way of some other similarly morally reprehensible behavior. So now, not only is this one lone successful person seen as an outsider, they are seen as being evil as well. If they try to remain within the group, they will actually lose social status and become an object of contempt or even hatred. This is of course a tremendous loss of social capital, and that is a terrible price to pay for the monetary gain that led to it.

And perhaps an even more important element is that some groups maintain connectivity almost *solely* through their shared negative experience. There is a subconscious acknowledgement that if the group's collective problems were to be solved, there would be no other connective element to maintain the group, and thus their most prized possession, i.e., their connection and belonging "wealth," as it were, would be lost. This means there is a tremendous incentive to maintain the negative experience. In such situations, anyone trying to better themselves or solve the problem is seen as the group's worst enemy.

This kind of cultural inertia is a most insidious element of poor kid thinking. It afflicts entire groups of people, making them believe that the only way to maintain the one thing they prize the most– a sense of belonging– is to give up everything else and remain poor. They actually take steps to make sure it continues. It is often done with the best of intentions, but even the power of love can be twisted by poor kid thinking.

19

Quid Pro Quo

Another reason poor kids find themselves pushing wealth away is that they may have experienced money coming to them with unreasonable conditions attached to it. You know, like that great aunt who spent a year knitting a grotesque sweater, and now you feel obligated to wear it, even though you can't stand it.

Every contract has elements of quid pro quo, and let's face it, some people may have "given" you money, and even though it may be ostensibly a "gift," there may have been an expectation that you will give them some kind of service in return. Perhaps that expectation is so great you can never give them anything of comparable value to get back to even. This is sometimes called "emotional loan sharking."

Sometimes this is inadvertent, sometimes it is intentional, and sometimes you may just be imagining it.

Now you may, at some point in your life, have encountered someone who willfully decided to cheat you. Sadly, such people do exist. Perhaps they took advantage of your vulnerability, and whenever they "gave" you any money, there was a bit of emotional loan sharking going on. Without realizing what was happening, you got yourself into a situation where you could never repay what that person claimed they had "given" you, as what they gave you was beyond the face value of the money itself; it was also the pain of their sacrifice as well. And now your sense of guilt and emotional imprisonment is not worth any amount of money they may have given you.

Again, we get into how important trust is when trying to go from poor kid to rich kid. If you run into this sort of emotional entanglement often enough, pretty soon you lose any expectation of fairness, and you default to just avoiding the possibility of ever letting it happen to you again. This is the principle of universal limitation being manifested once more. Rejecting offers of so-called gifts becomes a reflex. Rejecting cash becomes a way of managing personal boundaries, because if you accept any money, you lose the right to say "no" to that person. And so, when someone with good intentions and fairness of mind offers you money, you may presume, given your previous experience, that you are better off not having any money rather than accepting yet another unknown, and potentially infinite and virtually enslaving, debt of gratitude.

Money has no emotion, it has no conscience, by itself it is inert. It's like the ink in a printer, it will print whatever words, and thus convey whatever feeling, that we instruct it to do. Its only power is what we impart to it. It is easy to associate money with a bad experience, but that's like associating the floor with a bad experience. The floor was there, but it had nothing to do with it. Neither did the money. They were just there at the time. It was really about the energy being exchanged between you and that particular person. In another situation, a healthy generous person may be offering you money. It's a floor again, it's money again, but in every other way the situation is completely different.

If some sort of abusive behavior is going on, sometimes we don't want to have to look at that dead on. So instead we see the money as the culprit. This is like blaming your phone for the bad news you received today.

It is very easy to get one's personal boundary issues involved in how we deal with money. If past boundary incursions have made you suspicious of anyone offering to give money to you, you may be overly cautious about new opportunities, or you may be so concerned about avoiding endless potential bad consequences that the contract negotiations fall apart. Worse, you may be so eager to avoid any sense of indebtedness or gratitude that you limit what other people give you. This may keep away bad consequences, but it also prevents major windfalls from coming your way as well.

Every deal is different, so don't automatically push money away from you. It has no conscience. It has no feeling, it has no intention. It is neither good nor evil but that thinking makes it so.

One day the poor kid of our story got a job. It wasn't much, but it was money, and at the end of the week he got his first paycheck. He needed the money desperately, so as he got up to leave, he said to his new employer, "Thanks so much, I owe you big time."

The employer, who just happened to be a wealth minded person, actually stood up and challenged this poor kid's statement. "You don't owe me anything," he said. "I needed a job done and you did it. I paid you a fair amount. There is no more owing."

This statement came as a shock to this poor kid. He was not aware of it being possible to be "out of debt." One of the issues of being a poor kid is that people will take advantage of you and make you feel like you can never do enough for them. It is an emotional version of a "company store." You feel "worthless" because no matter how much work you do, it never seems to be enough. This is an awful state of emotional bondage and constant unhappiness. Good fences make food neighbors, and living in a world of mutual respect for personal boundaries, personal choice, and freedom is a big part of being a rich kid.

20

Manipulation of Desire

If the primary poverty-thinking concept of "desire is bad" was beaten into you when you were a kid, hopefully this discussion has started the process of rethinking the whole concept– or perhaps we should say, re-*feeling* the whole concept– of desire. Hopefully the poor kid approach of suppressing your desires, or otherwise being negative about your desires, has been addressed. That was step one.

The next step is thinking that desire is positive. Now that your desire is out in the open and not stuffed into the sock drawer, it now has to be managed as a resource and profit center. This means organizing, prioritizing, and focusing your desires. For poor kids, this is all new. Unfortunately, there is a lot of confusing information out there making it hard to stay focused. If you are new to getting what you want, this makes it that much harder. So let's examine the problem big picture.

You aren't the only one who has desire, of course. Lots of other people have desire too, and most of them have a desire to sell you something. Since desire and money are essentially the same thing, a lot of people have figured out that the easiest way to get you to buy something is to convince you that you desire what they are selling. This is done in a variety of ways, but one of the most common is to confuse you by associating an extraneous product that you don't want with something that you *do* want.

Most of the products marketed to us every day are not basic necessities. We can easily live without most of them. In other words, we don't really want them. So how can anyone convince us to buy them? Easy. They imply that getting these things you don't want is essential to the process of getting the things you really *do* want.

Most of the time, this consists of implying (while never actually stating) that buying this or that extraneous product will lead to greater social acceptance, personal well being, or even more likely, a combination of the two. (Again, we come back to this ongoing theme that the thing we want the most is connection. Most of us never get enough of it, and when we do, we are eternally worried about losing it.)

Perhaps the most obvious example of this system at work is your basic beer commercial. While some may disagree, beer is not essential to life . . . but that is hardly the implication of your average beer commercial. The ads never tell you that it is even a choice. They make you want it. Desperately.

How do these ads do this? Well, just one example, there was one recent beer commercial that showed an average young guy bellying up to a bar, behind which stood an absolutely gorgeous young woman. Now in that situation, for the guy in the ad, and for every insecure lonely young man watching the ad and projecting themselves into it, the woman is a whole lot more desirable than anything else in the room. So the obvious path of the mind is to immediately start figuring out ways to achieve greater connection with her. Once that desire is established, the young lady behind the bar (and oh my god, she is gorgeous) makes it clear that in order for the young man to be seen by her as an acceptable mate, or for that matter, to be seen as being socially or sexually acceptable to any female (or even socially acceptable to the other guys), *there is a condition*: the young man must demonstrate his acceptability by choosing the right brand of light beer.

Now bear in mind, getting back to our true core desires, being socially acceptable is not an option, it is essential. It is our greatest desire. And the fear of being disdained by anyone, of any sex, is so great that we panic easily. In that desperate panic, all logic is tossed to the winds, and thus we fall into the intended conclusion of believing that we must drink this or that brand of beer to be socially and sexually successful.

This is not true of course, but the story looks real, the gorgeous babe behind the bar looks real (she isn't, by the way), so why take the chance? It's only a couple of bucks. Set 'em up.

If this scenario was presented to you on a conscious level it would immediately be seen as ludicrous. But of course, the whole point of advertising is not to make cogent arguments, but to *create desire where there was none before*. And the easiest way to do this is to take an existing desire, i.e., the desire for connection, and make the product seem like an essential item for expediting your achievement of that goal.

And thus we create what can best be described as "desire inflation." We start to think that we want lots of things that we don't really want.

People have a right to make a living, and one single beer ad is not going to cause the downfall of western civilization, but there is a broader issue here: It is the cumulative effect that this kind of advertising has on society. Its collective impact is to be a relentless assault on your fragile individual sense of being lovable and socially acceptable. It places tremendous emphasis on conditional love. It endlessly paints a picture of a world that is harshly judgmental of you, while very little emphasis is placed on how eager other people are to be accepted . . . by you.

Young people in America often suffer from a chronic fear that they are not intrinsically lovable or sexually attractive. This is not a surprising situation. Every personal product advertisement they see preys upon, and magnifies, their emotional vulnerability, and implies that they currently lack some essential attribute of being socially acceptable or lovable. It is sales by a thousand cuts. Young adults are repeatedly told that achieving their greatest desire, i.e., connection to others, can only be accomplished by purchasing some recently devised product, even though, at this time of their lives, on a purely physical plane, they are perhaps the most attractive they will ever be in their entire lives.

There are literally thousands of advertisements for various nonessential products, all designed to rechannel your core desires, and make you confuse your true core desire (for connection) with desire for anything and everything, from makeup and hair coloring to exercise videos, from clothing to cars. These advertisements, made by experts who apparently have no conscience, all make the subtle implication that if you do not purchase these products, you will be rejected by your peer group and by your preferred potential sex partners.

None of us are all that terribly certain of our social acceptability, and so we are in a constant state of hyper vigilance about it. We worry about what other people think of how we look, how we smell, what we do for work, what we wear, how we stand, what we eat, what we drink, where we went to school. We wonder if something is hanging out of one nostril. All the while, we are being told by third parties that the people we most desire are secretly and harshly judging us, and we are assaulted– yes, that is the right word– with doubts and fears and implications that what we intrinsically are is simply not good enough. We are not desirable, not lovable, not acceptable, *unless we buy* . . . .

A major problem with our overly productive society is that we need to induce an enlarged sense of desire in everyone in order to keep the factories going and to keep people employed. We are just so darn productive we need to get people to buy more than they need or really want. Sadly, this leads to the marketing people constantly piggy-backing onto our true desires, which, while necessary, tends to dilute and misdirect them.

To be truly wealthy is not just to have money. Real wealth can best be defined as having that which you truly want. While for most of us this is primarily having a state of connection, how that is achieved is different for everyone. The point is, *to get what you want you need to know what you want*. And if you are getting confused about what you want, and you are buying a lot of stuff that you don't really want, you may not have time, money, or space for the few things that you really really *do* want.

It's easy for the one big desire to get drowned in a sea of lesser ones that are easier to fulfill today. But if you don't have the things you want the most, you are poor, no matter how much stuff has accumulated in your house.

So to be a rich kid, always ask yourself before you buy: do I really want this, or is this just a second-rate substitute for what I really want?

21

Desire Management: Scavengers

If you have ever had to take care of an infant (or perhaps someone's sick cat), you have probably had the rather vexing experience of this infant or sick cat being upset. Of course, when this happens, you want them to stop crying, so much so that you will give them whatever they want, if only you could ascertain what it is that they want. You offer them this, you offer them that, but nothing seems to satisfy them.

This scenario often plays out within ourselves. We sometimes feel a vague longing for . . . *something* . . . and we know not what. We know that this vague feeling means that we want something, and we try everything from chocolate ice cream to a spa treatment to satisfy it, but sometimes the longing relentlessly remains, unidentified and unsatisfied.

Desires often come to us in the vague pictorial language of the subconscious. For example, we may think our desire is to win the Nobel Prize, when it could be that all we really want is for our parents to appreciate our modest achievements. In other words, we don't always know exactly what it is that we want.

So far this book has talked a lot about desire, but instead of just talking about the expression of desire, this chapter is more about the concept of desire *literacy*. It's about the art, science, and skill of knowing precisely what you want. The more specific you are in knowing your desires, the less time you will waste on wild goose chases of things you don't want as much.

This is one more dimension in which rich kids have so much of an advantage over poor kids.

Rich kids generally have the opportunity to experiment with and refine their vocabulary of desires. They can buy something, and if it turns out that's not what they really want, it's not the end of the world. They can just throw that item away and go get something else. After a while, they learn how to interpret desire and act on it more judiciously.

For poor kids, it's very different.

It's hard for poor kids to develop basic desire literacy, because it's really hard to know if you truly want something until you actually have it. Very often we are led to believe that we want something when we really don't. After all, there are millions of people working at trying to make us think we want things that we don't really need or really want. They often imply that if we get this or that thing, it will immediately lead to our having what we truly want. Sadly, only too late do we notice the fine print, "Results are not typical."

Only when we have the object of this implanted desire in hand do we finally realize that no, we *thought* we wanted this, but it turns out this really isn't what we wanted, and it's not *getting* us what we wanted either. But for a poor kid, oops, too late. At this point the scarce available resources have been exhausted, so there's no chance to run a second experiment. There is no more money with which, through a continued process of elimination, to search for and discover one's true desires. (Added to this of course is the pain and embarrassment of realizing your naiveté has been exploited, again reinforcing a sense of universal negativity.)

Because really poor kids hardly ever get what they want or even have much of anything, they develop a survival mechanism, which is blindly grabbing "whatever you can get."

Even when you are talking about murderously poor kids, they don't live in a vacuum. There are always lots of castoff junk items floating about in their environment. You may not have any desire for a cowboy hat, but if you see one in the dumpster, you grab it and take it home. Who knows, maybe you really do want a cowboy hat, it's just that you never really had a chance to think about it. Better to grab what you can get and at least have something, as something is better than absolutely nothing. It's not what you wanted, but it's better than not having anything at all. It's there if in case someday you do want it.

This kind of fumbling-in-the-dark desire illiteracy leads to a kind of "scavenger" mentality. You stop thinking in terms of defining a specific path towards your greatest desire, and instead accept the "fact" of constant scarcity, and you learn to just grab at whatever leftovers float by, or whatever other people have left out on trash night. You are programmed to always grab what is cheaply or freely available. Desire is generally bad, but it's okay to want this stuff, because no one else wants it. And one can trust this kind of possession, because no one will steal it from you. This is, again, because no one else wants it. For a kid starved for any kind of trust or desire fulfillment, this isn't much, but it's something.

Again, we discover how poor kid thinking can so easily become self-sustaining, as a total lack of focused goals and desires leads to simply meandering from one garage sale to another, hoping for a random encounter with what one truly wants. A similar approach is taken to career development, passively "waiting for one's ship to come in." Odd jobs are taken "for the money," not for any other purpose-driven reason.

There are many people who will buy things on sale, even though they have absolutely no need, desire, or use for them. But, for a very low price, now you at least have something. It's not something you want, but, it's something; and having something, even if it's not something that you want, is a whole lot better than having absolutely nothing.

The trouble is, clutching at random objects that happen to be available right now distracts one from determined focused effort. The useless junk accumulates, taking up space that would be better left empty for the moment when useful stuff becomes available. One's life becomes cluttered with static interference that distracts from ever finding one's true desire. The desire is there, but no one knows exactly what is desired, and so like the unknown desire of a crying baby, you toss random things at it hoping it will satisfied with them, but it never works. This is a sad, and common, symptom of poor kid thinking.

The fix for this, like lifting 300 pounds, is simple but not easy. One must refute poor kid thinking, specifically, the false belief that you cannot have what you want. You must no longer see your true desire as being just a source of painful frustration. You have to believe that fulfillment is possible even though you cannot currently see any way of getting there. You must no longer believe that the way to get through life is by suppressing true desire. You have to stop getting through life only by wanting what is easily acquired.

Rewiring the brain to believe otherwise, i.e., that what you want IS possible to get, even if for the moment it seems impossibly far away, is the challenge, but this is how rich kids think.

By itself, the believing is not really hard. It's the undoing of the "unbelief" and cynical doubt that is so hard. Since the belief in impossibility was created by yourself as a means of protecting yourself, you may feel a certain fondness for it. But now that you understand how poor kid thinking was created in your mind for a now obsolete purpose, hopefully it will be a little easier to weed it out once and for all. You can now get on with getting what you want the same as everyone else, and you can forget that you began this life a few yards back from the starting line.

22

Desire Deferment

Poor kid thinking is filled with many falsehoods designed to cover its true structure, which is largely one of fear, resentment, and pessimism. One of the most common false beliefs of this system is the sincere belief that all this negativity and suppression of desire will actually somehow lead to success and wealth. In poor kid thinking, it is assumed that by suppressing the "evil" of desire, you are being noble and virtuous; therefore, someday your virtue, sacrifice, and loyalty to the poor kid thinking system will be rewarded with your desires being fulfilled . . . either by Prince Charming, the lottery, or some other outside entity who will actually force success upon you.

This approach to success is not entirely insane. After all, if you were adrift in a lifeboat in the middle of the Pacific Ocean, this approach would make sense. You would want to keep all effort and consumption at the barest minimum, as you wait for someone else to rescue you. But most of us are not in a lifeboat in the middle of the Pacific Ocean. In real life, you should defer desire into the future (and not act on it today) only if there is a good reason for doing so.

Desire deferment is often just a lie told to your subconscious. This is a very bad habit. If you have a real desire to go to, say, Venice, you should not address that desire simply by saying "Someday I will go." Endlessly deferring your trip to Venice off into the unspecified future date of "someday" is the same as denying yourself that trip. It is poor kid thinking at work, disguised as a good intention. Believing that you can't have it *now* is the same as thinking you can't have it *at all*. Since you cannot have it *now*, when "someday" comes, well, that someday will be a Tuesday very much like today, so when that moment comes it will be "now" as well. And since you never seem to do or have anything *now*, you will never go, period.

Now maybe you don't have the time or money right this minute, but you can still act on your desire and begin the process. There is more to going to Venice than just getting on the plane. You *can* plot your itinerary, you *can* start to research hotels, you *can* apply for a passport, you *can* read books on the subject, you *can* do the budget. These are all things that are essential to taking the trip, and they don't cost very much money, so what's your excuse for not doing them right now, unless you really don't want to go? Again, there's that pesky word *want*.

Fact is, somewhere deep down inside you probably do want to go (and you really *should* go), but poor kid thinking constantly tells us to suppress desire, and deferring your want into the future is a very good way of suppressing desire without admitting to it or realizing it. Also, by making a false promise, it makes you think something is being done and all is being taken care of when it isn't. It makes one think it will an easy thing, when in fact even a fun trip like going to Venice requires all kinds of planning and preparation.

Of course, the real issue here is not one of logic but one of emotional energy, both good and bad. Going from a state of suppressing desire to a state of acting on your desire will unleash a lot of pent-up sadness and pain, and issues of past fear and mistrust will grind in your guts. Poor kid thinking is, amongst other things, a kind of anesthetic. If you stop thinking like a poor person, you will become conscious of the lifelong backlog of checkout-counter candy frustration. It can be a terrible life passage, but it is worth it, and there is no other way.

So from now on, to be more like a rich kid, well, don't be rash or impulsive, but on the other hand, never defer your desires unless there's a good reason for doing do. Sure, you can shift your desires around, and sometimes you have to wait, but if you are deferring satisfaction of a desire, there should be a productive reason for it. Deferral of desire should be for a strategic reason, not just a policy of habitual suppression of desire. It's also a bad habit to tell lies, even if it's just to yourself. Again, poor kid thinking can lead you to believe that chronic self denial will, all by itself, get you a reward. You now have permission to question this idea.

Fulfillment of life's grand desires is hard to predict. No matter what your grandest dream adventure may be, it will never be totally practical, it will never be without cost, it will never be perfect, and there will always be a reason not to go. But time is limited, and, as Shakespeare noted, "We shall ne'er be younger."

*   *   *

One of the biggest pitfalls of poor kid thinking has to do with what you *deserve*.

Poor kids are famous for coming up with methods of rationalizing the pain of unfair circumstances, and the phrase "I don't deserve it" is a classic example. If you don't "deserve" it, well, now it makes sense that you didn't get it. The sense of injustice is not so irksome any more.

Of course, there is a flip side to not deserving good things, and that is, the bad things that have happened to you that you didn't deserve either. Did you "deserve" to be born into a difficult situation? Are your parents' personal shortcomings something you "deserved"? No. Good things and bad things happen to everyone, and to paraphrase Clint Eastwood, "Deserve's got nothing to do with it."

Thinking in terms of whether or not you "deserve" a better job or a nicer apartment is a major obstacle, because like so much of poor kid thinking, it becomes an invisible hand that holds you back from seizing opportunity. If you think you don't "deserve" to live in a clean house, even though it is well within your power to make it happen, you have hypnotized yourself into thinking it cannot be done.

There is no "Bureau of Deservement" determining standards of "deserve." Like permission, your "deserving" something is simply an arbitrary decision about how you will direct your emotional energy today. Deserving is not always getting, but if you think you *don't* deserve something, you may reject it out of guilt without even noticing.

So, here is some homework for you: Start saying to yourself "I deserve [x]", where "x" is something you don't yet have. It can be a thing, or it can be money, love, good fortune, a clean kitchen, whatever. When you feel that you are entitled to something, you are much more likely to go after it full throttle. This will hopefully serve to counter the embedded-in-your-subconscious anti-wealth poor kid belief that you don't "deserve" to be a rich kid.

And another bit of homework, which takes a little more effort: Just as a 20-minute daily experiment, imagine that you already have the thing, situation, or wealth you long for. Instead of saying "I wish all my bills were paid," say to yourself, for a few minutes each day "All my bills are paid . . . now what?" By thinking of wealth as a present state instead of a future state, you are far more likely to manifest wealth itself than you are by constantly thinking about how poor you are, and all the apparent hurdles between you and wealth. You don't need to have the actual dollars in the account today to at least make yourself feel "rich" for a few minutes. If nothing else, it's good practice for when the dollars finally get here, and if the physicists are right, such positive energy and imagery is far more likely to manifest wealth than will your creating constant "emotional resonance" with fear and scarcity. Your emotions have just as much substance and energy as the 1's and 0's in a bank's computer, so which comes first, the numbers in a bank account, or the emotional state of embracing a state of wealth?

23

Cutting off One's Nose to Spite One's Bank Account

There is an odd form of insanity abroad in the land these days. It is a form of poor kid thinking that has become so prevalent that it is overcoming the consciousness, and simple common sense, of the majority of our fellow citizens. It has to do with the terribly shameful activity known as "lavish corporate junkets."

In the midst of the recent "great recession," well, not everyone was broke. Some folks, including some bankers and managers at various other Fortune 500 companies, still had lots of money. So whenever one of these large companies ever put on some sort of "lavish corporate junket," their desire to spend some money and have some fun was seen as the work of the devil himself. People ended up screaming at their congressmen about how disgusting and unfair this is. And so, to avoid the fallout of the bad press, many companies simply stopped putting on these events.

Okay, so far so good. It is understandable that we might feel envious of people who have enough money to throw lavish corporate junkets in the Caribbean. But if we step back from this, we see the awesome power of poor kid thinking at work. As is always the case, poor kid thinking always looks terribly righteous, but it always results in making everyone poorer.

In this case, well, okay, we had one small victory here. We managed to momentarily suppress some of our pain by making some fat cats go without too. We stopped them from making us feel even more envious, because we managed to keep them from spending and enjoying their wealth as much as usual. To poor kid thinkers, the act of helping to create universal limitation feels like justice and righteousness.

But this is all denial and illusion. If you really and truly want to see wealthy people have less wealth, one of the best ways to achieve that goal is to get them to spend some of it. These "lavish corporate junkets" cost a lot of money, and furthermore, all that lavish corporate junket money goes to people like, well . . . you and me. Every time a "lavish corporate junket" gets cancelled, this impoverishes endless numbers of cab drivers, bartenders, wait staff, event planners, hotel staffers, airline pilots, and entertainers. So who gains anything by this suppression of desire? Nobody.

And by the way, these "lavish corporate junkets" are not vacations, they are sales meetings, and the only way to attract really well-heeled customers is by doing something wildly lavish enough to make them want to leave their wildly lavish mansion homes in order to attend. And when they buy, it is to do ever more big projects that ultimately employ more and more people. Suppressing marketing and commerce, just because the people involved may be having fun doing it, is crazy. And poor kid thinking is crazy.

24

Synthetic Poverty

There is another kind of poor kid thinking, one that can be a little hard to comprehend. This is the kind of poor kid thinking that afflicts people . . . . who have a lot of money.

Yes, believe it or not, it is quite possible to have a lot of cash on hand and still be dirt poor.

People who suffer from poor kid thinking but who still have plentiful cash on hand get negative results, even with the cash. They are not to be envied. They apply the tenets of poor kid thinking to their lives the same as regular poor people, but they actually make it worse by magnifying it with cash.

For example, the only pleasure they get out of wealth is through someone else's suffering. Instead of connection, they seek a sense of disconnected superiority. It is truly sad to see someone who already has millions of dollars, yet they can't be happy unless their "golden parachute" is bigger than their next door neighbor's. This is a bizarre form of poor kid thinking, in that their only pleasure is derived, not from having more, but from another person having less, although in this case "less" may be having only 20 million dollars instead of 30 million.

The next thing many poor people with cash do is, they fear that there won't be any more cash coming in, so they spend as little of it as possible. They wear worn out clothes, they drive a junk car, and they keep the heat at 62 degrees all winter. They have all the money they need, but you wouldn't know it by how they live or by how they treat themselves. They may as well not have any money; their daily lives would be essentially the same without it, although if they lost the money, they would be somewhat richer, for their lives would not be filled with worry about losing it. If they lost it, they might even rediscover the wealth of providing meaningful service to others, and maybe have some friends again too.

Perhaps the best example of synthetic poverty is the disproportionate wealth you see in many third world countries. People who have excessive amounts of cash in these societies certainly have many advantages and comforts, but at the same time, they are not free to walk the streets in broad daylight. They are virtual prisoners in their gilded cages; they live in constant fear of kidnapping and home invasion. They spend their money building more and bigger walls, and hiring more and more security guards.

If you have accepted the poor kid thinking belief that interactions with other people will always be negative, that the whole world is always trying to hose you, that all interactions involve a winner and a loser, if you fail to see that money is just a reflection of desire and is not intrinsically good or bad by itself, if you believe the only reason anyone wants to see you or take care of you is because of your money and not because of your shared innate humanity, and if you are unable to trust anyone, well, no matter how much cash there is in your bank account, you are dirt poor. You suffer from poor kid thinking.

25

Time Is Not Money

When Benjamin Franklin said "Time is money," he meant that one should be constantly moving towards new opportunities, and not dawdle in one's pursuit of success. In the industrial age, this has come to mean something completely different.

In the beginning of the industrial era, many jobs consisted of repetitive physical or mechanical work, so it was easy to measure that work over an hour, and then determine the commodity value derived from it. For example, one can calculate how much coal the average coal miner can dig in an hour, and thus determine the "value" of that person's time by the price of that coal. This presumption, that the amount of time spent on the mechanical aspect of a task translates to a specific amount of money, is a limited and now obsolete idea.

If you have ever met a billionaire, you will notice that they seldom seem to be in very much of a hurry. That's your first clue that time is not money. After all, if time is money, shouldn't billionaires be frenetically buzzing about the room? And here is another clue: let's suppose you have a piece of information that, if I had it myself, I could immediately make a million dollars. And let's also suppose that it would take you ten minutes to share this information with me. In this case, what is your "time" worth? It's a silly question, because time is not an issue here. The value of your million-dollar information is worth at least a few hundred thousand dollars. How does that relate to your "time"? Answer: it doesn't.

Poor kids are taught to think of work, even "brain" work, in mechanical/physical terms, and that it can all be measured, bought, and sold in increments of time. Some people are so steeped in this mechanical thinking that they assume they should get paid for their time as though their time itself has value. It doesn't.

Yes, you can make money working per hour, but the real question is not "how much time did it take to do this?" The question is, "how much value did you provide?"

There is nothing wrong with charging by the hour, in fact most people do, but this artifact of the industrial era is inherently limiting. If you are charging by the hour, that means you are providing a commodity service that can be measured by, and is perceived to be, a series of physical actions. If you have ever wondered why some people make $10,000 a day, it is not because of how "hard" they worked or how many hours they put in. It's because of the value, real or perceived, that their customer received. The value of their "time" transcends any mechanical measurements.

Poor kids have great difficulty in seeing themselves as having value beyond mechanical measurements. They also tend to see money in physical/mechanical ways instead of it being a representation of the ethereal and infinite energy of desire. Rich kids do not suffer from this self-imposed limitation. Time is limited for everyone, but money is infinite. If you relate money to time spent doing a task, you are accepting universal limitation once more. Value is just another word for desire, and desire has no limits. If you have enough money, you can hire people to shorten the time it takes to do a job. If people really want something, money, and time, are no object.

26

The Poverty of Time

While we tend to think of poverty as the scarcity of money and the material goods it buys, there is another kind of poverty/ scarcity that is not generally recognized as such, and that is the modern scarcity of free time.

Question: How much time in an average day do you "own"? That is, how many hours of the day or week are there in which you have total command and ownership, and freedom of choice? For many people working 60 to 80 hours a week, not very much.

We are virtually inundated with "time-saving" devices and systems these days, but for all the time we "save," who has a largesse of time any more?

For all the "wealth" we possess in terms of cash on hand, in terms of "wealth" as expressed by how much of our time we own and control, we live in a culture that is time-impoverished to the point of destitution.

Like many people who live in a state of poverty, people who are "time poor" tend to see themselves as helpless or even noble victims. The lack of time seems like an inevitable problem of our era, but like so many poor kid thinking problems, we make it ourselves. In this case, time poverty, like monetary poverty, exists in part to shield us from pain. Again, the one thing we want in life more than any other is connection, and if real connection is lacking in our lives, having a "wealth" of time becomes a source of pain. Why? Because if we ever slow down long enough to examine our situation, we risk being reminded of just how poor we are in the realm of interpersonal connection. Being time poor, like all other forms of poor kid thinking, distracts us from things that are too painful to bear. We cannot have a "refusal experience" of connection if we have no time to spend with anyone in the first place.

Where time poverty is concerned, we rationalize our lack of time by taking pride in our collective ability to survive and cope with the privation . . . Just like poor people do with money poverty by seeing themselves as being morally superior to the idle rich.

Time is wealth, and if you don't have any time to do things you want to do, like maybe sleeping, relaxing, or travel, you are not rich, no matter how much cash you have. Of course, if you don't spend time on things you want to do, are you suppressing your desires, and using lack– in this case, lack of time, not money– to rationalize your choices? Or to manage your personal boundaries?

Creating a constant sense of time shortage is a kind of illusory wealth, in that, if you are constantly behind schedule, it is easy to take the idea of "supply and demand" and twist this around into thinking that this lack of your time is because there is a greater desire for you. This almost makes sense. But if your time is so scarce that you are constantly frustrating the desire of all the people who want to see you, you see how the "limited amounts of everything" doctrine of poor kid thinking is really holding sway here. You are actually creating scarcity, in this case, of yourself. So you are in essence creating poverty experiences for people, especially for those closest to you. And you are creating poverty for yourself if you are managing your time in such a way that you never have any of it left over.

Granted, if you lack time, then there is also a lack of time for bad things like loneliness and boredom to occur. In this way, many people use time poverty to avoid buried fears and bad memories, just as the money-poor use poor kid thinking to avoid pain as well.

27

Poor Kids, Money, and Fear

Since money is really just a numerical reflection of the emotion of desire, it might be useful to examine another powerful emotion that affects our view of money, and that is . . . fear.

Poor kids generally experience a lot more fear than rich kids. In poor kid schools and neighborhoods, there's a much greater probability of being exposed to violence, and of course there's the fear of all the many unpleasant things that can result from not having any money. And if that weren't enough, there's also the general fear of the potential shame and embarrassment that comes with having one's lack of this or that exposed to peer group ridicule.

Fear is a natural reaction to stress or danger. It is there to help you survive a difficult situation, either by helping you to keep very still, or by helping you to run away. But like so many poor kid survival techniques, something originally meant to address a problem often ends up perpetuating it. So let's take a look at the emotion of fear.

Emotional energies work very much like many other forms of energy, in that they have positive and negative polarities. Fear has two polarities. If you observe any squirrel, you will quickly see these two polarities at work. There is the "frozen stiff" polarity of fear, and there is the "panicked and running as fast as you can" polarity.

We tend to think of fear as an independent emotion, but in fact the primary power of fear is how it affects the general flow of our other emotional energies. Fear has the effect of making other emotions accelerate or slow down. It's like the pedals in your car. One pedal makes your emotions go faster, the other pedal makes your emotions come to a halt . . . a screeching halt, if you step on the pedal hard enough. Since money is based on emotion, fear has the same power over the flow of money. It either makes money flow way faster than it should, or way slower . . . or stop the flow altogether.

Since fear can lead to a faster flow of emotion in the form of spending money, there are lots of people who use fear-inducing sales tactics. You are no doubt familiar with the exhortation that you must "act now," as something terrible will presumably happen if you do not buy a product immediately. You know all the sales pitch clichés – "Ends at midnight," "going out of business," "everything must go," "closing our doors forever," "this is the last one."

And then there is the opposite situation, where fear makes you freeze. Sometimes you really should spend your money on some necessity, but your vague feeling of fear makes you stop and do nothing.

We often use fear to regulate behavior, either our own or someone else's. It's quick, easy, and effective. The trouble with using fear as a regulator of emotional flow is that it tends to affect the entire spectrum of one's emotional energies, not just one or two channels of it. People who live with fear are always either very jumpy or unable to move at all. Most people fall into the latter category. They lead lives of "quiet desperation," not allowing emotional energy to flow, for fear of some bad consequence that may occur. But inevitably the emotional energy builds up, and the dam bursts briefly, often resulting in binge spending, or in bingeing, period. (Some people can only feel alive when they are drunk. The alcohol temporarily removes the fear that is inhibiting the normal flow of emotional energy.)

The "freezing" polarity of fear has one very practical application: if you have had a lot of unpleasant experiences, you can use fear as an anesthetic to slow or even deaden the flow of those painful "feelings." However, there are two problems right off the bat: first, by suppressing the bad feelings, you end up letting them fester instead of allowing a natural healing process to occur; and second, to achieve this anesthetic effect, one must constantly maintain the fear by ruminating on fearful thoughts. For poor kids, this usually doesn't take very much imagination. In fact, for some people, this habit is so ingrained that it takes far more effort to *stop* dwelling on the fear-inducing thoughts than it does to constantly dream them up.

But again, when you deaden one channel of emotion, you deaden all of them, and this means the emotional energy of desire is deadened too. Therefore the flow of money is deadened as well. The fear of having no money can actually be a cause of having no money, as money is based on the flow of emotion, mostly that of desire.

Along with the anesthetic effect of frozen fear, the "panic" polarity of fear also has many uses, mostly as "motivation." If you can induce enough panic in yourself, this will result in a massive burst of effort. The trouble is, it is not sustainable. You eventually get used to the fear, or you realize things are not as disastrous as you thought. In either case, you eventually run out of adrenaline and fall back into frozen fear mode, where nothing happens and you have to sit and wait for the next disaster to inspire some fear-based panicked action again.

When trying to seek motivation to act, there is a big difference between using panic-based fear and using purpose-based passion. Rich kids don't use fear as motivation. They move in one direction towards something good, not in every direction away from something bad. They allow emotions to flow more freely; they don't bottle them up as the answer to their problems. They can sustain effort over longer periods because they are not constantly grinding internally against exaggerated thoughts of negative possibilities that must be run away from.

To get in touch with your inner rich kid, you want to remove as much fear from your life as you can. You may feel that you cannot achieve anything without the accelerant drug of fear, but this is poor kid thinking. People who believe that fear is the best motivator assume there are limited amounts of everything, including their own persistence, determination, and ability to face their problems.

Fear is a part of life. You can't get rid of all of it. You may not be able to do much about the presence of axe murderers down the street, but you can certainly take steps today to not think about imaginary worst case scenarios that create more fear than you already have.

28

Poor Kids and Limitation of Solutions

You may have occasionally come across these little humor postings on various websites, which feature unusual test answers given by little kids. One such test answer featured a geometry problem, where the length of one side a triangle was marked with an "x." The test asked the student to "Find 'x'." So this little kid had drawn a little arrow pointing at the x, and he had written, "It's right here."

So here is the question for you to ponder: is this really a "wrong" answer? After all, what is "incorrect" about it? He found "x." It was incorrect only because it was not the one single answer someone in authority was expecting. And the next question is, why is there only one correct answer so much of the time?

In schools everywhere, there is a tremendous emphasis on there being only one correct answer. This kind of training can lead to a common state of poor kid thinking, i.e., that of universal limitation. In the entire infinite universe, does every problem have only one single correct answer? That's a pretty limited approach. Yet we train people to think this way constantly.

The idea of there being only one right answer flies in the face of what we know of the physical universe. The universe is infinite, and that infinity includes an infinite number of solutions. In fact, there are probably more solutions than there are problems.

So when you get an unexpected bill, or some other calamity befalls you, well, ok, the "answer" or "solution" may not be immediately apparent to you. Disaster may seem imminent, and the answer that others have proclaimed as the only correct one may seem impossible to achieve. Well, perhaps that one "right" answer is unavailable, but the notion that "there is only one correct answer" is a form of poor kid thinking. And just because you can't see another right answer right now doesn't mean it doesn't exist.

One reason why the solution to a problem is not appearing may be because you are so obsessed with finding just one pre-existing specific answer. Don't limit your mind. Don't think of the universe as a highly sparse limited space with a limited number of anything. All scientific data refutes that notion. Believing in limitation of correct answers (or limitation of anything else) is poor kid thinking.

29

Poor Kids, Rich Kids, and Food

Okay, here is an honest to goodness true story of a poor kid coping with the issue of food.

Once upon a time there was a poor kid who had a major conundrum regarding peanut butter. You see, he did not like it. At all. But he was a lost "middle child" somewhere in the middle of six kids, and every day this poor kid's mother would simply slather some peanut butter onto six slices of white bread, cover each glop with another slice of bread, toss it into a paper bag, and that was lunch. For his entire year of first grade, he had to force down a peanut butter sandwich. Every . . . single . . . day.

So summer came and went, and a new school year began. This poor kid sat in his second grade classroom, dreading the approach of lunchtime. He could not help but ruminate upon his facing yet another year of legume-based slow culinary torture. But then, a most interesting thing occurred: his new teacher made a casual announcement that "all the kids whose parents have prepaid for the year for hot lunches, just get in line."

This school did, in fact, offer up a daily hot cafeteria lunch for any kid who could scrounge up a quarter to pay for it. To this poor kid, to have a quarter every day seemed like being as rich as Croesus, although he didn't really know who Croesus was. In any event, this poor kid was also something of a black-sheep wise guy, and so, in an inspired bit of intended troublemaking, he thought he would go stand in the prepaid rich kid line and have some fun when he got caught for clowning around.

Well guess what. No one was paying any attention. He was just waved along in the line, and he had himself a fabulous non-peanut-butter hot lunch, with all the trimmings.

So the next day he tried it again, and whoosh, into the line he went, no questions asked. It had never occurred to anyone that some seven-year-old might hatch a plot to embezzle $40 worth of chipped-beef-on-toast, on an installment plan no less. Also, the cashier just got used to seeing his face in the prepaid group (all of whom, by the way, got to go through the line ahead of everyone else). Nothing was said.

The cafeteria ran on a staggered schedule, so none of his siblings saw him doing this. It was the perfect crime.

Well, it was almost perfect. There was one little problem: what to do with the paper bag, and the unwanted legume-based nourishment contained therein?

We should again point out that this kid was something of a black sheep. He had taken on the role of scapegoat in his dysfunctional family dynamic, if you can follow that sort of John Bradshaw-esque terminology. If you don't well, in any case, he had to be very careful to not get caught, as he was "the usual suspect." So to keep up appearances, he had to leave the house each day with the lunch bag in hand, but once he was in the school, what to do with it? He had to quickly and quietly get rid of the legumus delicti, otherwise someone might get suspicious and the whole thing could come crashing down on his poor little seven-year-old head. And in an elementary school, there are finks, snitches, and tattle-tales everywhere. What to do?

Well, this poor kid's school building was very old, vintage 1880. Instead of lockers, each classroom had a cloakroom, with two open entries at either end. The building had extremely high ceilings, and this cloakroom had a system of high wooden shelves, going up above twelve feet and more. Due to the narrowness of the cloakroom, it was impossible to see anything on these high shelves without actually fetching a ladder and climbing up to gain access to them, so they remained largely unused.

The poor kid saw his chance. Each day, as the class bell rang and all the other students bolted to their desks, this lone poor kid would be alone and hidden from view in this cloakroom. And he would emulate an ancient Greek discus thrower, as one, two, threeeeeee, he would heave this unwanted bag of ground peanuts and white bread into the upper shelf regions of perceptual oblivion. Gone. Let's eat.

And so this ritual repeated itself each and every school day. He would leave home with a lunch bag, he would conceal it on the bus, and then at the precise bell-ringing cloakroom-and-dagger moment, he would heave it into the stratosphere. And each day, this poor kid would then chow down on the cafeteria's wonderfully varied hot lunch.

All seemed grand and glorious, as autumn turned to winter and then to spring. But then, one Monday morning near the end of term, the kids filed into class after the year's first truly warm weekend. At that moment, it was clear to everyone that something was rotten in Denmark.

The smell. Good heavens. It was like a punch in the face.

After the initial shock, there was a great deal of highly entertaining excitement. The teacher summoned the assistant principal, who then summoned the principal. He in turn stood there trying to decide whether he should call the fire department, a hazmat team, or perhaps the city morgue, as the smell could have easily been ascribed to the presence of a dead body somewhere in their midst.

At last, cooler heads prevailed, and someone had the presence of mind to call the janitor. He wandered about, finally ascertaining that the smell was strongest in the cloakroom. Unable to see what was on the high shelves, he fetched a ladder. He climbed up, looked around, and in a most inappropriate use of language in front of a large class of seven-years olds, exclaimed, "WHAT THE HELL??!"

For there, strewn all higgledy piggledy on these high shelves, were more than a hundred paper lunch bags, each containing a peanut butter sandwich in its own unique state of moldy decomposition.

Everyone looked around with astonishment. Our poor kid hero did his best to look more astonished than anyone else. "My goodness," he asked, "where do you suppose they came from?"

He never got caught. He kept that story a secret for 40 years. And those hot lunches were delicious.

This story is shared with you for a number of reasons. First of all, it's just a fun story. It also illustrates how, when poor kids are forced to cope with an unfair world, they sometimes exhibit extraordinary creativity and daring. But for now, we will limit ourselves to one single aspect, which is the topic of poor kids, rich kids, and food.

When it comes to poor kids, rich kids, and food, we face a bit of a puzzlement. One would think that, since rich kids have so much more money than poor kids, rich kids would tend to be fat and sassy, while poor kids would tend to be gaunt and underweight. However, a cursory glance at the statistics shows the opposite result. How can this be?

The topic of food and psychology is far beyond the scope of this book, but when we talk about desire and the suppression thereof, one of the most consistent manifestations of desire is hunger. And when you live in a poor kid thinking world, desire is bad. That means hunger, that is, the desire for food, is bad as well.

So again, you might think that "desire is bad therefore hunger is bad" would lead to poor kids not eating anything. Sometimes that is the case. But while poor kids may be poor, they're not stupid, and as you have seen, they often come up with remarkable workarounds. If the desire for food is bad, well, one of the best ways to suppress hunger is to simply eat constantly, thereby never allowing oneself to get hungry in the first place.

When you look at the typical ways food is marketed to poor people, there is tremendous emphasis on the speed of access to it. In a poor kid world, it is very important to suppress desire as quickly as possible, so speed of delivery is certainly a major draw. A large volume of food is also a major draw, as this means it will be that much longer before any hunger returns. This makes sense, sort of, except when you consider the miniscule nutritional value of this fast/junk food. (Purely from a marketing perspective, the speed, volume, and low price have to be emphasized, as the overall nutritional value is so low. And by the way, the seemingly fabulous limited-time low-price offer is there to keep you from taking the time to ponder this.)

As poor kids grab at the foods that are readily available and they can afford, they believe they can quickly end the dreaded feeling of desire, but then, the opposite happens. No matter how many sugary snacks they consume to chase away the feeling of hunger, the low nutritional value and the high amounts of sugar tend to make one feel ever greater hunger, rather than satisfying it. And then the cycle just repeats and repeats.

Another issue is purely one of taste. If you want to preemptively remove your hunger, this means you have to eat when you aren't hungry. The only things that can override the body's natural sense of satiety are the extreme tastes of salt, sugar, and fat. It's very hard to stuff down kale or string beans when you're not all that hungry, but salty chips and chocolate desserts, you can scarf those down even if you're already stuffed.

*   *   *

By the way, when our poor kid hero went to the rich kid school, there was no more bringing bags with sandwiches. There was no standing in cafeteria lines with trays, either. Everyone was assigned to a table that was headed up by a faculty member. Students rotated on a schedule of acting as waiters, bringing trays of food to the tables. This meant that, most of the time, these rich kids experienced lunch as something that was served to them, in essentially unlimited quantities.

To this poor kid, this daily rich kid dining experience was fantastic in and of itself, but then . . . but then . . . it went even further into the realm of fantasmagorical.

This rich kid school had a deal at the end of each semester, where regular classes were suspended and faculty members taught two-week "mini courses." These included everything from beginner golfing to photography. And in one such "mini-course," this poor kid found himself at the French teacher's house, every morning for two whole weeks, taking a course in . . . French cooking.

Each class started with the kids making omelettes for breakfast. Then they would spend the morning laughing, chatting, and cooperatively preparing a sumptuous lunch, which featured such dishes as coq au vin (special permission was granted by the state board of education for

138

them to consume wine-based sauces– it didn't hurt that the French teacher was married to a state senator), escargot, beef bourguignon, and crepes suzette. Before taking this class, this poor kid had never seen fresh garlic, he had never eaten a green vegetable that hadn't come from the freezer, nor had he ever even seen a mushroom that hadn't been packed in a can. It was a whole new culinary world.

When you eat food that is satisfying on an aesthetic and social as well as a nutritional level, when you eat food that is not made up largely of salt, oil, and sugar, you tend to eat only as much of it as your body really needs.

So here is the lesson: as you get in touch with your inner rich kid, remember that a big part of being a rich kid is eating like one.

You are worth the time and the money. Your physical health is your most valuable possession, and food and your health are inextricably linked. Do what you have to do to maintain this wealth. Be aware that there are large numbers of people (with large advertising budgets) who are trying to persuade you to eat things that you don't really want. And don't feel that you need to stuff yourself with food that's here today because you're afraid that there may not be any food for you to eat tomorrow. That is "universal limitation" poor kid thinking at work. It's also a lack of trust, another classic attribute of poor kid thinking.

Nutritious food does not have to be expensive. And in the process, let yourself have the desire of hunger. Everything, even kale and tofu, tastes better when you allow yourself to get hungry before you eat it.

Hunger can be very confusing for a poor kid. This is because hunger is a powerful desire, and as you know, for poor kids, desire is bad. This gets ever more difficult for poor kids, as there are many forms of hunger. Poor kids hunger for nutritional sustenance, but they also hunger for things like emotional sustenance, and the wiring for these signals of desire is often intertwined. Therefore it is easy, and quite common, for poor kids to get them confused.

For example, when a poor kid feels a desire for some love and attention, they know that a very painful "refusal experience" is likely to follow. What to do? How can one suppress this vague longing and make it go away? For a poor kid, a quick remedy is to shove something– anything– down the throat, and hope it hits the empty spot.

Note, this grab for quick food is not done to satisfy the desire for love and attention. Quite the opposite, in fact. To a poor kid, desire is bad, so the eating here is not done to satisfy the desire. It is done to suppress the desire, or at least distract oneself from it.

Reaching for the chocolate ice cream or the bag of chips is a vain attempt to stop the desire in the first place, as a full stomach might spill over and make the heart not be hungry any more either. Or maybe the pain of a stuffed stomach might distract you from the pain of an empty heart.

Bear in mind that this is all poor kid thinking, of trying to avoid the pain of a refusal experience by somehow eliminating desire. To become a rich kid and get what you want, you must start by no longer telling yourself the catechism of lies that poor kids are taught to repeat every day, such as "you don't deserve it," "you can get along without it," or "this is all there is, and there won't be any more." Being a rich kid is about having what you want. And you *can* have what you want. You may not be able to get it right this minute, but even there's no sign of it on the horizon, it's still okay to want it. The first step in getting what you want is letting yourself want it.

30

Poor Kids, Rich Kids, Anger, and Power

Of all the many emotions that money represents, having money also has another emotional attribute, and that is, it represents a feeling of . . . power. It is easy to feel that if you don't have any money, you don't have any power either.

One can argue back and forth about just how much power money gives you. After all, some very poor people have wielded enormous influence over civilization. But those notable folks aside, yes, for the average person, the less money you have, at least in the temporal realm, it sure can feel like the less power you have as well.

So how do poor kids deal with having less power? Simple. As is so often the case, they gravitate towards a cheap and readily available substitute. And for poor kids, that substitute is . . . anger.

A sense of anger is a delicious, if illusory, sense of personal empowerment. When one is in a state of anger, one can easily feel that one has much greater physical power, not to mention far greater powers of persuasion. It is easy to think that, when one is in a state of rage, the extreme emotional energy one is exhibiting surely must have the effect of garnering greater support for one's cause. And if one is angry, there is a presumption that one is angry because of a good and righteous response to some evil energy. Even without the feeling of power, that sense of anger-induced moral superiority is delicious all by itself.

So what is anger?

Anger is a natural reaction to a state of feeling powerless. If you find yourself being cornered by a saber toothed tiger, it can be very helpful to go into a wild rage, as your only chance of survival is to bluff the tiger into thinking you are dangerous. However, when trying to mediate a dispute, or manage anything, anger is worse than useless.

Here is the core of the problem: anger is a powerful reaction to feeling powerless. Therefore, if you if you only feel empowered when you are angry, well, the only way you can induce this anger-based sense of empowerment is to meditate on how powerless you are (and how overwhelmingly powerful your opponent is). Do you see the contradiction? You simply cannot make yourself feel truly empowered by constantly meditating on how powerless you are.

Another major downside of anger is its addictive qualities. Anger is habit forming, in that it just feels good. It can easily become a default response and "fix" to everything.

If you have an anger "habit," this is not entirely your fault. Our popular culture endlessly encourages anger. For example, there is an entire genre of movies that indulges the desire for anger-based power fantasies.

These movies all have an exceptionally simple and highly repetitious form, consisting of three simple characters: 1) an omnipotent "bad guy" who has no redeeming features whatsoever, 2) a nice, easy-going, blue-collar, working Joe who seeks peace and quiet and wants no trouble, and 3) a helpless and vulnerable small child (or very chaste young female) who is threatened with imminent harm by bad guy character #1.

The horrifically nasty behavior by the bad guy, especially when juxtaposed with the total innocence of child/chaste female #3, now makes it necessary for easy going Joe #2 to turn off the ball game and address the bad guy's awful behavior. Even though nice guy #2 is willing to put up with any amount of physical abuse himself (because he is oh so tough, patient, and mature), once the sweet little vulnerable party #3 gets threatened, well, stand back. Easy going good guy #2 has been pushed too far, and now, in the last reel, he gets . . . angry. And that anger empowers him to serve up some seriously righteous and well deserved bad guy smackdown justice. Once the good guy has been driven to a state of anger, oh my, vigilante justice, torture, and murder are all justified.

Of course, if you take a moment to look through all this, and if we can refrain from indulging in the delicious sense of righteous rage, we quickly realize that in real life there are few, if any, truly omnipotent bad guys. Also, the ultra-innocent vulnerable children in these movies are really the vulnerable bruised spirit in all of us.

One reason this kind of anger incitement can be so overpowering is that we identify so much with the helpless victim. You may have some buried memories of being mistreated by people who had power over you long ago. When those ancient feelings are dredged up, it is very easy to be completely overwhelmed by the anger reaction, and thus lose all self control or common sense.

Like so many other forms of faux wealth and power sold to poor kids, anger being a means of acquiring power is largely an illusion. It actually serves to make you weaker. If anger created actual power, you would see people with actual power utilizing it. Instead, they seek to make other people angry, because by *not* being angry, and by making *other* people feel angry, they acquire *real* power.

Rich kids rarely get angry. If they get bothered by something, they don't fly into a rage. They fly into action, or they fly into their lawyer's office. Anger is an unfocused and generally wasteful loss of energy. To go from being a poor kid to a rich kid, you have to seek your real power. This means giving up on the illusory power of anger. Anger and confidence are mutually exclusive emotional states. Like optimism and resentment, you cannot feel both. You have to pick one or the other.

Making you angry is a common form of manipulation, or even oppression. Be on your guard for anger incitement. Anyone who seeks to make you angry about something will always claim to be serving the greater moral good. They will appear to be serving your personal interests by exhorting you to react with rage to some act of extreme injustice. But if someone is seeking your support on an issue solely by demonizing someone with an opposing viewpoint, they are trying to do an end-run around your calm rational mind. By trying to incite a knee-jerk reaction on your part to a highly simplistic black-and-white version of the problem, and not making a calm logical argument, they are seeking to take you out of a realm of your being in a state of *empowerment*, i.e., of calm thoughtful self control, and into a realm where you are out of emotional control, i.e., angry. And if they succeed in making you angry, you are powerless.

Anytime someone encourages you to be outraged, this should set off an alarm in your head. By making you angry, they are making you lose control, making them more powerful, not you.

If you have been a poor kid, there are probably a great many memories of past injustice, as well as memories of being bullied, abused, or otherwise feeling powerless, that you are thoroughly justified in being angry about. But trying to fix it with anger will get you nowhere. Anger will actually serve to keep you in perpetual poverty, possibly more than any other aspect of poor kid thinking.

To be like a rich kid, decide today that you will no longer indulge in anger-based fantasies of empowerment, and you will start to seek real power through calm deliberate action. Anger is ugly, and will always serve to drive resources and people away from you. Instead, calmly and patiently seek consolidation of your network of friends and allies. When someone suggests that you should be outraged by some third party's actions, check the facts before reacting. And always look for an ulterior motive. Whenever you lose control, someone else inevitably gains it.

Tantrums are for children, and while a tantrum can occasionally get some short term concessions from those in power, it is very hard to maintain that energy for very long. All the non-tantrum-throwing party has to do is basically sit and do nothing, and wait for the tantrum-throwing party to exhaust themselves. It's an easy win.

Despite what the movies imply, there is nothing manly (or womanly) or noble about not being able to control one's emotions. The people who don't get angry are the ones who have all the power.

*　　*　　*

One of the greatest responses to poor kid thinking is the "Four Way Test" of Rotary Clubs International:

Of the things we think, say or do:

Is it the TRUTH?

Is it FAIR to all concerned?

Will it build GOODWILL and BETTER FRIENDSHIPS?

Will it be BENEFICIAL to all concerned?

31

Reinstating Trust and Removing
Universal Negativity

One of the best things you can do today about poor kid thinking, one that will significantly lower your sense of universal negativity as well as begin the process of creating more trust, is fairly simple: Start thinking very critically about what "media" you allow yourself to watch.

Even if you are a poor kid, people are still eager to get you to tune in to their TV show. Ratings are ratings, so everywhere you look you can find television and radio programs that fully resonate and reinforce a poor kid world view, of universal negativity, limitation, and total lack of trust. It's appealing, almost hypnotic, because it feels just like home. Let's start with "the news."

Now this is not to suggest that you should stop watching the news or become a total ignoramus about world affairs. It's important to have an informed electorate and have everyone up to date on current events.

But here is the problem with . . . "the news," or at least the news offered by the commercial networks: it is a nonstop lesson in not trusting anything. Unless we landed someone on Mars today, the top story of every newscast will always the biggest trust violation that occurred on planet earth today. For example, we all like to trust Mother Nature, but if she recently exerted some highly unusual record-setting wrath on one single town in Oklahoma, even though it was beautiful weather everywhere else in North America today, that's . . . the news. The ground is pretty stable most days, but if it shook violently somewhere, that's . . . "the news."

Tens of thousands of dedicated mayors and city councilpersons sit in boring meetings all over America every week, trying to fix the potholes and balance the school lunch budget, but if just one of these people gets caught with their hand in the till, that gets featured on . . . "the news."

The fact that these negative events are statistical outliers is seldom mentioned. In terms of corrupt politicians, "news" about them contains a subtle implication that all politicians are like this, and these are just the ones that got caught today.

One news series, "The Fleecing of America," featured a regular series of reports on instances where we, as taxpayers, were being routinely taken advantage of by someone in government. These kinds of "here's how your vulnerable self was viciously abused today" news items are yet more lessons in non-trust; these reports may seem like well-intended information, and they seem like disparate unrelated events, but when you take it all together, the vast majority of "news" stories like these are, in some way, an assault on your childlike rich kid belief that the world will work in a kindly honorable trustworthy fashion today.

Here is some alternate "news" for you: Every year in the United States, billions of dollars are given away to charitable organizations, by well-intended fellow citizens, for the purposes of making our lives better. Many of our most important cultural and social institutions were founded by people who sought to make this world a better place. But this kind of honorable activity is never on the news (unless, of course, someone on the board of directors gets caught with their pants down. Then it's "news.")

Now along with your trust being corroded by reports of the worst disaster du jour, there is also all the universal negativity reinforcement via the nightly television entertainment of mayhem and murder. By one report, an average American child will see 200,000 violent acts and 16,000 murders (mostly staged, but some real) on TV by age 18.[2] That's a thousand murders a year. (That seems low. If you watch two *Law and Orders* and a *Star Trek* rerun, you will see about eight gruesome staged deaths. If one did that every night, it would add up to almost 3,000 staged murders a year. This says nothing of the carnage of violent video games.)

Even the comedy shows are always about some negative thought or premise. Every program is about an unworkable problem, a trust violation, or an unresolvable interpersonal conflict.

---

2   Senate Committee on the Judiciary. Children, violence, and the media: a report for parents and policy makers. September 14, 1999.

So again, just as an experiment, take a few days and simply avoid modern "entertainment" and "the news." If something on the news is important enough, people will come up to you and start telling you about it. Otherwise, you can get through life without knowing about it for a few days. Try to get a "balanced" view of the world, not by listening to the rants of rightists and leftists, but by protecting your fragile spirit from the constant onslaught of trust violations and graphic violence.

As stated previously, trust is key to acquiring wealth. A presumption that the world is a generally positive place is key to acquiring wealth. The systematic destruction of your sense of trust is a form of economic oppression. You are strongly advised to not let this kind of overblown pessimism and trust destruction enter your thinking.

We do, of course, need the press to act as a watchdog on the all too corruptible people who serve in positions of power. But if it's all one sided, if we constantly corrode our trust in our fellow citizens and in our civic institutions, and we never have any building of it, then we are moving toward living in a world without trust, and the absence of trust is a sure sign of poor kid thinking.

32

Poor Kids and Loyalty

No book on the emotions of money would be complete without addressing the emotion of loyalty.

Loyalty is a powerful force in human affairs. No matter where you go on this earth, wherever you find human beings, you will find expressions of loyalty, be that to a political leader, a religion, a school, or a sports team. People who work in marketing often speak about "brand loyalty." Once we pick a certain brand of car, beer, or computer, we are likely to stick with that brand for the rest of our lives. It's just the way we are.

Again, when we speak of what we want the most, at the top of the list is a sense of connection, i.e., belonging and community. A major element of your "belonging" to a group is your loyalty to that group, and that means being obedient to that group's values, dogmas, and world view. To question these things would be disloyal, and that would result in your expulsion from the group.

Loyalty is tough to overcome, because the mere act of being loyal, even to something that is totally nonsensical, carries with it an immediate emotional reward of a sense of belonging. In fact, the more irrational a group's beliefs are, the more of a sense of belonging one's loyalty creates, since "belonging" is that much harder to do in terms of stifling your common sense. .

If you have invested your loyalty in a society of poor kid thinkers, you have a serious problem. The more irrational their poor kid beliefs are, the more intensely the group members will defend them.

So when you start to question and challenge the poor kid thinking you may have been taught, you must prepare yourself to face the issue of loyalty. To start, there is your own loyalty; thinking like a rich kid may make you feel like some sort of traitor or criminal. And then there is the collective cultural loyalty of the many people with whom you feel your greatest connection. The group is likely to see your strange "rich kid" ideas as being a major threat to the group. Like you, they are also extremely loyal to their cultural system and values, and if they are poor kid thinkers, there is no easy fix. Their loyalty to these ingrained poor kid beliefs cannot be undone by rational argument alone, as the emotion of loyalty tends to overwhelm logic.

Worst case, you may have to simply leave that community behind, and lose your precious wealth of a sense of belonging therein. But think of it this way: if you are truly loyal to these people, if you truly love them, then it is incumbent upon you to take action, be courageous, and show them a good example of a better way. This is, in a way, a sign of even greater loyalty.

If you have ever wondered why poverty lasts through multiple generations, why it defeats so many government efforts to eradicate it, or why the "sins of the fathers" are passed down through multiple generations, it's not that people are "dumb." You are witnessing the emotion of loyalty overpowering logic.

33

Pecking Orders

Whether you are talking about chickens or wolf packs, pecking orders are a part of the natural order.

Pecking orders are key to group survival. Once they are established, pecking orders keep internal group strife to a minimum. When a wolf pack brings down an antelope, pecking orders determine, in advance, who eats first, thus keeping the group from wasting precious energy on internal squabbling.

Pecking orders also apply to primates, and that includes us. Seeing the way pecking orders apply differently to poor kids and rich kids a major element of moving from being a poor kid to a rich kid.

Now, one would think that the pecking order is pretty obvious here—the rich kids are higher up and the poor kids are lower down. The end. But that is not what our poor kid observed in the rich kid school. The rich kids transcended the whole concept of pecking orders.

The most obvious instance of this has to do with standardized tests. As stated earlier, in poor kid schools, there is a passion for testing and grading and rating and ranking and testing some more. There is a fascination with reducing each poor kid to a uniform generic being.

But at the same time, the test scores are then used to create a pecking order. It is openly and clearly announced who did better than whom on these tests, and this becomes the overriding statement of who you are in this poor kid society. The pecking order is paramount.

Conversely, in the rich kid school, not only was the standardized testing kept to a minimum, it had no bearing on social status. Grades were not ABCDF, it was a "pass fail" system, thus everyone seemed, on the books anyway, to be virtually equal. It was an absence of a social ordering system that, let's face it, is an attribute common to animals.

The rich kid school placed tremendous emphasis on unique individual capabilities, unlike the poor kid school, which was all about comparison of generic low level commodity capabilities. It's hard to have a pecking order between a rooster and a pickup truck. Since there is no similarity or comparison, there is no conflict.

While we can never get totally away from the pecking order instinct, it is still a low on the brain stem bestial instinct, and thus needs moderating. That said, since the poor kid school was a more bestial place—more violence, more fear—pecking orders played an important role in mere survival.

In the rich kid school, however, there was transcendence of pecking orders. Again, like trust, it was not immediately apparent; one had to piece it together from the evidence. The strangest thing this poor kid observed was how many of the teachers preferred to be addressed by their first names. This would never happen in a poor kid school, where the fragile higher pecking order status of the teachers and staff was paramount, and not to be questioned for fear of physical beatings.

And of course, just as wolf packs have only so much antelope meat to go around, in a poor kid world there are finite amounts of everything, and so pecking orders become key as a way to disburse the minimal resources available. In a rich kid world of abundance, pecking orders were unnecessary, and so they just faded out of social functionality. The constant insults and put-downs of hen houses and poor kid culture were absent, because they were unnecessary.

But here is the magic trick: it is key for a poor kid to see that pecking order fighting is counterproductive. When constantly pressed with pecking order conflict, people become very defensive, ready to explode on the slightest inkling of an impending challenge to their fragile sense of social rank. For the rich kids, they inherently understood that pecking order challenges either drive people away from you, or turn them into your enemy, and so, the kinds of constant put downs and insults that chimpanzees, wolves and poor kids do to each other are absent in rich kid culture. It is far more beneficial to not incite competitive defensive reactions in others, as the wealth to be derived from cooperative interactions with others is far greater than anything that can be gained via a short term fist fight at recess.

If you look at the vituperative comment threads so prevalent in social media, you will see one overriding ubiquitous element contained therein: it is always a kind of pecking order battle, between people who are very low in the overall social order trying to climb just a few inches higher by insulting another weaker poor kid. They may gain a short term sense of satisfaction or success, but in the process, they are making themselves so ugly and isolated that the energy of wealth, which generally comes through others in reaction to your gracious glowing loving energy, is denied to them.

It may seem counterintuitive to think that by not fighting for dominance over others in your immediate group you would gain higher status, but as the Bible teaches, he that humbleth himself shall be exalted.

34

In Praise of Your Poor Kid

So far in this book we have been fairly critical of the "poor kid thoughts" that may have been lurking in your head. But now it's time to show a little appreciation for them.

Fact is, those poor kid thoughts were once your best (and perhaps only) pal in the world. The reason that your poor kid consciousness came into being in the first place was to help you survive a difficult situation. That poor kid in your head loves you with all its heart, and was willing to go without pretty much anything and everything in order to protect you and help you to survive. Friends like that are hard to find. And if times ever get hard again, you can bet that your inner poor kid, and his ability to both suppress desire and to defer wants into the future, and to just generally act as a hyper vigilant protective sentinel, will be there to save you yet again.

Trouble is, your poor kid mind only knows how to deal with adversity and scarcity. It doesn't know how to create abundance. That isn't its job.

We are not suggesting that you abandon or discard your poor kid persona. Far from it. Why would you ever want to abandon an entity that loves you so much? Instead, let's think in terms of re-assigning him/her.

Your poor kid came to managerial prominence because at the time they did so, your inner rich kid was not yet ready to take on the job. That has changed. You are now big enough, strong enough, and wise enough that your rich kid mind, however vulnerable and needy it may be, can now step up and take over the task of managing your life.

So you need to sit down and have a little talk with your poor kid self. You should thank them for keeping you alive, and doing the best job they could with what they had to work with. But it is now time to stop asking this poor kid to do a job it's not at all suited for. You must tell your own rich kid self that it's time for him (or her) to trust in the goodness and infinite abundance that the universe is eager to give you. It is time to for your inner rich kid to step forward, believe and trust in himself, and take charge.

35

Apotheosis

If you think of your financial situation as an airplane, there are many people who will encourage you to fly higher by increasing the thrust of your engines. While this can have a positive effect, there is another way to fly an airplane to higher altitudes. You simply take a look in the cargo hold, and if you find an anvil or a grand piano, you simply remove it. Once you lessen that useless weight, it's way easier to fly higher and faster without working any harder.

That, in a nutshell, is what this book has been about. It has not been about how to make more money, but simply an attempt to draw your attention to the possibility that perhaps you have been taught to push money away from you.

Just a little reminder here: you were born a "rich kid." There is no such thing as a three-month-old baby who sits in their playpen asking, "Do I deserve to have my diaper changed? Are there enough diapers to go around? Can I trust anyone to do it right?" As newborns, we just naturally ask, expect, and trust. People only think like "poor kids" because they were trained to do so. It is learned behavior, and thus it can be unlearned.

It is sincerely hoped that by identifying the many categories of poor kid thinking, you can more easily recognize these habits and thus take steps to eradicate them.

Good luck, and we wish you all the best as you get back in touch with your "inner rich kid."

Getting in Touch with Your Inner Rich Kid
© 2013 Justin Locke

For more, visit

www.justinlocke.com

www.ingramcontent.com/pod-product-compliance
Lightning Source LLC
Chambersburg PA
CBHW021157010426
R18062100001B/R180621PG41931CBX00012B/19